"Dorothy Day's accomplishments were as vast as a continent; to grasp them requires a guide. Let it be Patrick Jordan, who dwelt with Day and their fellow Catholic Workers in the mystery of poverty. No one is better than Jordan at explaining the moral principles that woke Day up in the morning and led her to do battle with the world. He takes the reader into the adventure of Day's spiritual life, her jailings in the cause of peace, and the crossroads moment when she decided that, from then on, she would give of her soul and substance to the 'wretched of the earth.' And how she calls us to do the same."

—Jim O'Grady, New York Public Radio
Author of *Dorothy Day: With Love for the Poor*

"In Patrick Jordan's portrait, an inspiringly authentic Dorothy Day springs to life. The energetic-but-searching young journalist finds her adult vocation as a joyful prophet. In the author's view, Dorothy's faith is both a gift and hard-won, the result, for example, of living with the poor, nonviolent resistance and protest against injustice. Jordan's privileged position as a close friend, neighbor and co-worker   ʳothy for twelve years becomes a boon to every reader   and uncommonly mature reflection."

—Karen Sue Smith, former Editorial ʳ

"I love this book. It makes me feel   .othy Day in her lifetime, as Patrick Jc   .ceptive observations and deep knowledgᴜ   .e captures Day in all her inspiring, saintly contᵣ   .e tells a story that is at once witty and precise, movinᵦ   ₋oncise. It will appeal not only to those who know of Day and want to reflect further, but to those yet to discover her and the great meaning her life holds for us today."

—Paul Moses, author of *The Saint and the Sultan: The Crusades, Islam and Francis of Assisi's Mission of Peace*

Dorothy Day

Love in Action

Patrick Jordan

LITURGICAL PRESS
Collegeville, Minnesota

www.litpress.org

Cover design by Stefan Killen Design. Cover illustration by Philip Bannister.

All the Way to Heaven. The Selected Letters of Dorothy Day. Edited by Robert Ellsberg. Marquette University Press © 2010 and *The Duty of Delight. The Diaries of Dorothy Day.* Edited by Robert Ellsberg. Marquette University Press © 2008 Milwaukee, Wisconsin, USA. Used by permission of the publisher. All rights reserved. www.marquette.edu/mupress

Scripture texts in this work are taken from the New Revised Standard Version Bible © 1989, Division of Christian Education of the National Council of the Churches of Christ in the United States of America. Used by permission. All rights reserved.

1   2   3   4   5   6   7   8   9

Library of Congress Control Number: 2015936997

ISBN 978-0-8146-3703-6   978-0-8146-3728-9 (ebook)

For Kathleen: *Deo Gratias*

Contents

Preface

As part of the People of God series, *Love in Action* is an
introduction to Dorothy Day, one of the most challenging,
inspiring, and interesting women of our time. It is not a
traditional biography but a set of reflections and recollections by someone who had the good fortune to meet and
work with her during her final dozen years.

My wife Kathleen and I met at the Catholic Worker in
New York City in 1969, where we worked at St. Joseph
House and helped edit the *Catholic Worker* paper. From
1977 on, we lived on Staten Island in what was known as
the Spanish Camp, across the path from Dorothy's beach
bungalow. There we often shared conversations, meals, and
drives with Dorothy and her guests.

There is no finer way to understand Dorothy Day than
to reflect on her witness—her love in action—and to encounter her challenging, prophetic, beautiful, and disarming
words. This book relies heavily on both as well as on the
recollections of others. Dorothy was indeed salt for the
earth, a light for our days.

A personal note: I have been helped with this project by
countless individuals—friends, authors, and coworkers, the
living and the deceased—over the years. They include family, teachers, professional colleagues, and those who have

challenged and continue to inspire me by their "thoughts, words, and deeds." To each one of you, I hope my debt is evident in these pages. Be assured that any limitations or mistakes herein are mine alone.

(NB: In keeping with the era in which she lived, Dorothy Day's writings and utterances often made use of male pronouns, masculine references to God, and the term "man." But as she noted in her June 1972 "On Pilgrimage" column in the *Catholic Worker*, "When I write 'men,' I mean people.")

Introduction

It is impossible to do justice to a person's life in a short book—any person's—particularly when that individual has led a long, interesting, singular, and perhaps historic life. Should the person defy most established categories of success or even sanctity, the difficulty intensifies. Such is certainly the case with Dorothy Day (1897–1980), the twentieth-century American radical, journalist, and Catholic convert. In 1933 she and Peter Maurin (1877–1949) founded the Catholic Worker Movement, a radical pacifist undertaking for social reconstruction that has only continued to branch out and grow since her death.

Dorothy Day used to say she "wanted to wear out, not rust out," and while the last few years of her life were confined largely to Maryhouse, a Catholic Worker community for homeless women she had established in New York City, her presence was felt in every aspect of the movement's work—serving the poor on a daily basis and publishing a radical pacifist Catholic newspaper.

This reflection will convey a glimpse of what was singular about Dorothy Day, while not losing sight of her humanity. She was delightfully down-to-earth and a pleasure to be with—most of the time. As Stanley Vishnewski, a lifelong

Catholic Worker who died a year before Dorothy, observed with a characteristic twinkle in his eye, "once you got to know Dorothy Day, she was just like any other crabby old lady"— a fact that made her all the more human and appealing.

When my wife and I lived and worked at the Catholic Worker, just off the Bowery in New York City, Dorothy was in her seventies. I take it from others who knew her longer and earlier in her life that her seventies and eighties were a rather mellow period. Still, the 1960s and '70s were far from uninteresting times, and the challenges Dorothy faced— leading the Catholic Worker community, editing its newspaper, and being at times a controversial public figure in the antiwar, civil rights, and unionization movements of the day—demanded resilience, attention, and an uncommon wisdom. Added to this, she traveled almost incessantly during those years—from Indiana to India, Denver to Moscow, Detroit to Dar es Salaam—and corresponded tirelessly with family, friends, and readers. Picketing with farm workers who were trying to organize, at the age of seventy-five she was arrested and thrown into a California penal colony. Yet, for all that, when at home at St. Joseph House, she seemed totally present and at ease. You could walk into her room on the third-floor women's dorm at seven in the morning and find her in robe and slippers—her long, white hair not yet braided—as she shuffled into the kitchenette to prepare her morning coffee.

Dorothy was both the most self-reflective and consistently self-aware person I have known. I think she was probably more demanding of herself than the most gifted psychologists or spiritual directors ought to be. In part, this was because she was steeped in great literature, classical and contemporary, was a constant reader of the psalms and sacred Scripture, and understood that nothing escapes God's sight—in fact, that God's presence can be discovered anywhere, anytime.

A woman of passion and paradox, or as George Eliot described Dorothea Brooke in *Middlemarch*, "a sensuous force controlled by spiritual passion," Dorothy claimed in her classic, spiritual autobiography, *The Long Loneliness* (1952), that it was her love for Forster Batterham—her common-law husband and the father of their daughter Tamar—that opened to her the depths, riches, and enjoyment of not only nature but the life of the spirit. In a glowing section of that book titled "Natural Happiness," she describes everything she loved about Forster, including the sand between his toes when they climbed into bed together after a day on the Staten Island shoreline. She seemed to understand every aspect of human longing and the human condition. After her conversion, while always upholding the Catholic Church's teaching on marriage, abortion, and artificial birth control, she never denied the difficulties associated with them. For her, conversion and acceptance of those teachings came at a tremendous cost: separation from her husband and a life of continence.

Being around Dorothy could be challenging—and the church's sexual teaching was the least of it—for she was continually calling herself, others, society, and the church to task on a range of issues: war and peace, power, poverty, and material success. As an editor, she could be demanding of those who worked for her. Yet she was understanding and even apologetic if she overstepped in her criticisms. If she made a mistake in print or felt she had been unfair to someone in speech or action, she would typically acknowledge her failure.

There was a knowingness about her that stemmed from Dorothy's long years as a journalist and her place in the public arena. When you were with her, you had a sense there was little she had not seen or heard, either because of personal experience, work, or being associated with large and diverse groups. As a young woman, she had ministered to an acquaintance as he lay dying from a suicidal overdose and then concealed the evidence from the police. She told me she would bring an inebriated, shaking Eugene O'Neill to bed and get in to warm him up. When he propositioned her—asking if she would like to lose her virginity—she replied no.

When Dorothy did fall in love, losing her virginity was apparently not a grave moral concern. As she would say later, she flung her wild roses. When she recounted having had an abortion, she implied it was not uncommon in her circle at the time. Nonetheless, I sensed remorse, that her own awareness of sinfulness had reached an entirely different depth after her conversion. Despite confessing this deed, there remained in her a lifelong sense of its gravity. She was vulnerable to the reproaches of others on account of her wanton past, and at times was humiliated by those who relished throwing it up to her. As a young person, she had attempted suicide twice.[1] All these experiences, and the enduring sensitivity they brought her, led to an understanding of others and of human failure that could be liberating for them. In her presence you understood something of the profundity and limitlessness of God's forgiveness.

Dorothy had a sharp sense of irony, and it was occasionally writ large in her reporting and editorializing. Her sense of humor was not the jokey sort, but it included poking fun at herself and the pretensions of the Catholic Worker Movement. She liked to quote G. K. Chesterton that if something was worth doing, it was worth doing badly. She recalled that on one of her speaking trips, she was particularly tickled when an unexpectedly large group of undergraduates showed up for her talk "Saints and Heroes." It had been mistakenly billed as "Saints and Eros." Her daughter Tamar said she was a joyful person who always pointed out that the saints were joyful, and her laughter remained young and delightful to the end. Still, few photographs catch Dorothy laughing.

Dorothy seemed always happy to greet you—it went both ways—and could sit around a table for hours conversing with you or several others or a group, telling stories, going over the day's mail and news, talking about the next issue of the paper, and wondering aloud how so-and-so was doing at Bellevue or the VA Hospital. It was as natural as chatting together on the road to Emmaus.

On the other hand, Dorothy would occasionally make sure she was not seated next to an individual whose idiosyncrasies or self-importance she found tiresome. Then she would ask to be seated with her right ear (her nearly deaf one) next to the person. (Frequently, forgetting which one was her bad ear, I'd get in trouble for shouting into her good one.) Dorothy wrote in *The Long Loneliness* that God gives us our temperaments, and that despite her pacifism, it was natural for her to "stand her ground." Then she added that it was one thing to endure wrongs to oneself patiently, but that it was not right to patiently endure the wrongs done to others. As George Eliot observed of Miss Brooke, if she ever attained perfect meekness, "it would not be for lack of inward fire."

Ruth Collins, whom Dorothy encouraged to go into the real estate world so that Ruth could assist housing cooperatives in the poorer areas of New York City, said that "Dorothy could be very crabby on occasion"—for example, when a contractor failed to show—"but then she wouldn't think about it again." In contrast, Ruth said, she herself would still be mulling it over six months later. "Dorothy was so cheerful, so positive," Ruth said. If there was a setback in a project, Dorothy would say, "We'll just go ahead and do nothing; just go ahead and wait."[2] It's not the usual call to action you would expect from a fabled activist.

You never knew what advice Dorothy might come up with in response to a query or an observation. She seemed like the proverbial wisdom figure, bringing forth both the new and the old from her storehouse. You could always be sure, however, that whatever she said would be consistent with the gospels. Still, she was never simply a scriptural literalist, although she took the counsels of perfection to heart—the way she thought they were intended.

Dorothy may have had a deficient ear in older age, but she was a terribly good listener. Daniel Berrigan once remarked about "the ease of her attentiveness." Frank Donovan, who was Dorothy's devoted assistant during the last decade of her life, commented on how much information she could discover in a few minutes' time—an aspect of her journalistic skill—without seeming in the least intrusive. She had a retentive memory, capacious interests reinforced by her reading, and an eye for beauty. Fritz Eichenberg, the famed engraver and illustrator, said she had an intense love of beauty that included art of any kind. She also had a nose for fragrances, an ear for music—from Brahms to Joan Baez—and an eye for nature. She liked to repeat a line from the play *The Master-Poisoner* that her poet friend Maxwell Bodenheim cowrote: "I know not ugliness. It is a mood which has forsaken me."

If she spotted wild clover along a Staten Island roadside, she would have you stop the car, get out, and pick some. Then she would put it in the pillowcases in her bungalow—a practice, she said, she had learned from her mother.

Dorothy's mother came up in conversation often, usually coupled with some wise phrase or aphorism: "Dorothy bites off more than she can chew" or (when Dorothy or you had been subjected to someone's rash or critical judgment), "Never a lick amiss." In her autobiography Dorothy noted that there was little kissing in her family, only a "firm, austere kiss" from her mother each night. She was sure, she added, that this lack of expressive affection and her longing for it made her more intense, more sensual: "more conscious of the flesh which we constantly denied," creating in her a sense of conflict that "was to go on for years."

Dorothy could experience an acute sense of loneliness, and it was an important aspect of her awareness, from her earliest years. She and her older brothers used to play near the shore at Bath Beach, Brooklyn. From that stretch, facing the Atlantic, one can look southwest across the Verrazano Narrows and see Staten Island, which would come to play a significant role in her later life and conversion. But on one particular day in childhood, while playing alone, she had a sudden, acute sense of the vastness of the world and of the force of darkness. Only six years old at the time, the feeling was so strong she abandoned her play and ran home.

In *The Long Loneliness* Dorothy described another terrifying experience of being alone. It was during the 1906 San Francisco earthquake. She was eight, and her family was living in Oakland, California, where her father was working as a sports editor for a San Francisco paper. When the earthquake struck, he fetched Dorothy's two older brothers while their mother grabbed Dorothy's younger sister. Dorothy, the middle child, was left to fend for herself, in a brass bed that rolled back and forth across the floor. When she spoke of that sensation years later, it was as if it had just happened yesterday.

The same was true when she recounted another episode. It took place in 1905 in the cavernous St. Louis train station. For some reason, everyone else in the family seemed to disappear at one point, and Dorothy experienced a sense of frightening abandonment. She told this story to Kathleen and me many years later; it too seemed as if it had just happened. Even though she had many rich friendships, was the grandmother of nine and the founder of a large, widespread community, and was recognized in public and written about widely, in a very real sense she remained a singular, solitary figure.

Dorothy had a presence of mind that made you feel she was always "right there," even in unlikely circumstances. Father Thomas Goekler, a Maryknoll priest who worked for years as a missionary in Honduras and Guatemala, told the story of literally knocking her down one day at the Tivoli farm. It was the late 1970s. He was charging up the stairs when she happened to be starting down. "I crashed into her full force," he said, and "she went down like a ton of bricks." The priest was appalled, he told the *Houston Catholic Worker*: "This icon who had barely survived a heart attack or two was literally flattened. With great aplomb, she got herself up and steadied herself on the railing. She was a step or two above me and our faces were about the same height. She quickly leaned over and kissed me and said, 'A woman never stops falling in love.' That was the last time we spoke."[3]

Recalling her early, radical friend Elizabeth Gurley Flynn (1890–1964), Dorothy wrote that when you were with Flynn you experienced "the purpose of her life."[4] That could well be said of Dorothy herself. As the theologian and activist James Douglass noted, when you were with her "you had a real sense of grace in the way she looked at you, at people."[5] No one felt left out. Dorothy was there for *them*—for you.

As a result of this acceptance, you began to look at reality, your surroundings, and the people you lived with in a different light, and began to act a bit more nobly yourself. "The presence of a noble nature," George Eliot observed, "changes the lights for us: we begin to see things again in their larger, quieter masses, and to believe that we too can be seen and judged in the wholeness of our character."

This characteristic did not mean that Dorothy couldn't be short, overbearing, or even cantankerous. Jim Forest, one of her biographers, told a reporter in 1973, "She's not all sugar. She's tough."[6] And this included her stubbornness and holding grudges. She could also be impatient. Ammon Hennacy, who came to the Worker in 1953 and stayed a decade, recalled that when "some men in the office would ask her what to do about something, she would get angry and tell them to use their sense; if they made a mistake, that was how she had to learn and they could also." Perhaps her granddaughter Kate Hennessy has best captured her steel and the bracing aspects of her person: "She was fierce, dictatorial, controlling, judgmental, and often angry, and she knew it."[7]

By the time I knew Dorothy, she possessed what I would describe as an established "natural authority." It had been honed and proven over decades, and seemed to be taken for granted by the Catholic Worker community and others. When one possesses that kind of authority, it is bound to rankle some people, both in and outside "the family." Thus over the years Dorothy was tagged with a number of pejorative epithets: "the anarch," "the abbess," "the autocratic pacifist," "the queen," "the supreme matriarch." Occasionally, even reporters wishing to praise her slipped into such tropes. In 1973 a journalist for the *National Catholic Reporter* called her "the matriarch of the apostolate to the poor and the oppressed."[8]

Once, while out west visiting Catholic Worker houses, Dorothy remarked in an interview that she had been traveling to "give succor" to some of the newer communities. When word of this got back to New York, several younger members of the house greeted her choice of words with derision. The Catholic Worker Movement being an anarchist shop of sorts, by the time Dorothy returned home someone had painted a floor-to-ceiling mural on the third-floor landing. It depicted an Egyptian fertility goddess with a thousand and one breasts, fully exposed. It wasn't a bad representation of the deity, except for the head, which had been transformed into Dorothy's, featuring braided hair and all. A caption was included, to the effect that the goddess was "giving succor" to her minions. Dorothy couldn't have missed it—or its message. The mural stayed on the landing awhile and eventually was painted over. But in the end, it was the lack of a stormy response that was the real lesson.

Dorothy seldom capitulated. In 1937 when she had castigated Joe Ryan, the corrupt leader of the East Coast longshoremen, in a front-page broadside for his attempt to squelch the fledgling seamen's strike, the Catholic Worker's strike-support storefront window on Tenth Avenue was smashed with a paving stone. In the following issue of the paper, Dorothy answered: "We now have a new window—half the stone is used to bolster up our stove; and the other half is used to keep the bread knife sharp, as we are serving up to 150 loaves of bread daily."[9] Longtime Catholic Worker Marge Crowe Hughes once remarked that "Dorothy is not a saint. She's a warrior."

When Dorothy was jailed for the final time, her fellow inmates autographed her green prison smock, an act that pleased her greatly. "You know," she told a guard, "I hope to take this jail dress out with me when I leave. I know it's against the regulations, but I'm going to do it." And she did. (It's now at the Catholic Worker Archives at Marquette University.)

Dorothy seemed a person at peace with herself. Early on, in 1917, Agnes Boulton, who later married Eugene O'Neill, sized up the young Dorothy this way: "I saw at once this girl was a personality, an unusual one."[10] But that can hardly explain the eventual largeness of who Dorothy became or the peace that developed in her after many years of turmoil, wandering, and, as she would put it, "dying to self." By her later years, I sensed someone who loved life and happily wished to continue sharing it with others. Her writing often evinced a Pauline flavor. She could have written to readers of the *Catholic Worker* as Paul had to the Philippians in 4:4–7: "Rejoice in the Lord always. . . . Let your gentleness be known to everyone. The Lord is near. Do not worry about anything, but in everything by prayer and supplication with thanksgiving let your requests be made known to God. And the peace of God, which surpasses all understanding, will guard your hearts and your minds in Christ Jesus."

CHAPTER ONE

A Chronology

Dorothy Day's life story has been told often and well, probably nowhere better than in her autobiographical memoirs (*From Union Square to Rome, House of Hospitality, The Long Loneliness*, and *Loaves and Fishes*); her newspaper columns for the *Catholic Worker*; and her selected diaries and letters (*The Duty of Delight* and *All the Way to Heaven*). This book relies on these sources and others, quoting from them liberally in order to bring Dorothy's voice to the reader.

In person, Dorothy's speaking voice was young and could be lilting, even in her later years. While she often had serious matters to speak of, there was a liveliness and energy in her speech that conveyed not only her seriousness but also her wit, resolve, and sense of joy. You encountered something of the same qualities in her pale blue eyes. They were attentive, reflective, and could sometimes be on the verge of piercing; but they also had a twinkle and were not invasive.

To understand a person, it helps to have a sense of where he or she has traveled, not only interiorly, but vocationally and geographically. Following is a thumbnail sketch of Dorothy's peripatetic life.

Dorothy Day was "made in America." She had grandparents who fought on both sides in the Civil War. She lived in all four quadrants of the United States: east, west, north, and south, and understood America's people and its history.

She was born in 1897 on Pineapple Street in Brooklyn, New York, not far from the relatively new Brooklyn Bridge (opened in 1883). Brooklyn had not yet been incorporated into greater New York City. Today the area is known as Brooklyn Heights, a stone's throw from Walt Whitman's legendry Brooklyn crossing. (Later in life, Dorothy would come to know Hart Crane, the so-called poet of the bridge.) The delivery doctor was from nearby Montague Street, which half a century later would figure in the integration of American baseball when the legendary Jackie Robinson signed at the Brooklyn Dodgers' headquarters there.

Dorothy's father, John Day, was a sportswriter, and he and the family moved often. After a stay of several years in Bath Beach, Brooklyn, the family relocated to the San Francisco Bay Area in 1905. That move was the first of numerous cross-country trips Dorothy would make throughout her life.

When the Day family left California soon after the 1906 earthquake to resettle in Chicago (Dorothy's father needed to find work elsewhere because the printing plant for the paper where he worked had been destroyed), Dorothy fell in love with that city: its sounds and smells, ethnic neighborhoods, and parks. The family changed addresses several times, and by the time she had reached the eighth grade, Dorothy had attended five schools. In *The Long Loneliness* she paints a vivid picture of Chicago. She and her younger sister, Della, would push their baby brother, John, around the city in a stroller, exploring its avenues, parks, and even its stockyards. The Day children would often spend long hours at home, reading and entertaining themselves (all three of Dorothy's brothers would later become journalists). It was during this period that Dorothy first read Dostoyevsky, Jack London, Upton Sinclair, and Peter Kropotkin (the Russian "anarchist prince," living in exile in London, who had spoken in Chicago in 1901). All these authors had a profound effect on Dorothy and helped train her eye to focus on and understand the plight of workers, immigrants, and the poor.

In 1914 Dorothy matriculated at the University of Illinois in Urbana, aided in part by a scholarship for her proficiency in Latin. She spent only two years in college. She joined the Scribblers Club, wrote for the *Daily Illini* and the *Chicago Examiner*, and made crucial friendships with students who had radical and literary leanings. She seemed to take only those courses that interested her and eked out spending money by doing chores for professorial families. When her own family returned to New York in 1916, Dorothy was homesick for them and moved east as well.

At first Dorothy lived with her family, during which time she tried to find work as a journalist, despite the fact that her father was adamantly opposed to any woman setting foot in a newsroom. When she did land a modest job reporting for the socialist paper *The Call*, she immediately moved out and found a room in a boarding house on Manhattan's Lower East Side. In a real sense, she never returned home. In later years she would visit her mother, Grace, and her father, John, in Florida after they had relocated there, especially when Dorothy's daughter, Tamar, was a child. Following her father's death, she spent significant time with her mother on Long Island. She remained closest to her younger siblings, particularly her sister, Della. Her letters and diaries have many affectionate entries about Della (who worked for Margaret Sanger) and Della's family. During the years my wife and I were at the Catholic Worker, Dorothy often repaired to Della's for R and R. Over many years, Della would provide Dorothy with money for personal necessities and items like dresses and shoes.

The story of Dorothy's time as a young writer in New York seems drawn from a radical storybook. She wrote for cutting-edge leftist journals, explored life in the city, and caroused. She lived for a time with a Jewish family in a tenement walk-up on Cherry Street and came to have a lifelong appreciation for Jews, Jewish tradition, and Jewish theology. She was a close friend of (and for a period in love with) Mike Gold, the Communist newspaper editor whose 1930 tale *Jews without Money* became a classic account of New York's Jewish immigrants. Years later, Dorothy would relate the story of how Gold had saved a small, white-frame public library in Huguenot, Staten Island, in the 1920s. He had gathered the signatures to keep it from being shuttered, and it was still operating in the late 1970s.

Dorothy was in her late teens when she began writing for *The Call*. In 1917 she left the paper because of a misunderstanding with other staff members and began working for the more literary leftist journal *The Masses*. There she learned the art of editing, magazine paste-up, managing other writers, and meeting publication deadlines. She worked with such eminences as Floyd Dell and Maxwell Bodenheim, both of whom willingly handed over greater responsibilities to her. But this was all short-circuited when the United States government suppressed the journal in the fall of 1917 for the editors' opposition to American entry into World War I. By then Dorothy had been involved in antiwar demonstrations with the Anti-Conscription League in New York and Baltimore. She later remarked that, though she associated with both Communists and Socialists at the time, her pacifism had made her question class struggle as the best means of achieving revolutionary change.

Out of work and just turned twenty, in November 1917 Dorothy joined women suffragists picketing the White House. She was arrested and jailed for eighteen days. Back in New York, she moved from the Lower East Side to Greenwich Village, where she became part of a literary scene that included Eugene O'Neill, John Dos Passos, Malcolm Cowley, Hart Crane, Claude McKay, and later Katherine Anne Porter. But in a relatively short time, she decided to leave the Village to attend nurses' training school at Kings County Hospital in Brooklyn. She and some of her other Greenwich Village friends had been accustomed to welcoming homeless people they encountered, and after the suicide of a young friend, Dorothy decided to undertake a more serious and purposeful life. She also found herself inexplicably dropping into churches.

World War I was still plodding on, but closer to home a deadly flu epidemic broke out. Working on the wards proved a clinical testing ground for Dorothy. By morning, the long hallways adjacent to the wards would be lined with cadavers. This experience, coupled with falling heedlessly in love with a reporter, Lionel Moise, led to a turning point in her life: quitting nursing school to live with him and, subsequently, having an abortion. When Moise left her as he had warned, Dorothy undertook a rebound marriage to Berkeley Tobey, an older man of some means from the Greenwich Village crowd. The two set off for Europe: London, Paris, and Capri. During their year abroad, Dorothy read widely and wrote what would be her only published novel, an autobiographical story called *The Eleventh Virgin*.

By the time Dorothy and her husband returned to the United States in 1921, their marriage had dissolved. She set out for Chicago in pursuit of her former lover, who had moved there, and found work with *The Liberator*. Eventually she realized Moise was not going to return to her. It was during this time that she was arrested at a hostel run by the Industrial Workers of the World. She had gone there with a sick friend when, suddenly, the police broke in and charged her with prostitution. Her second experience in jail was far different from the first. This time she was jailed as a common criminal, not as a protester and the member of a high-minded, well-off group. Her second arrest opened a crucial door in her understanding, dramatically altering her perception of the American justice system and how it demeans those it snares.

After Chicago it was back to New York and an assortment of jobs—clerking and retail—and then in 1923, another relocation, this time to the Deep South and New Orleans. There Dorothy lived near Jackson Square and the St. Louis Cathedral. Along the way, a friend had given her a rosary. In New Orleans, Dorothy found herself praying it without knowing how to use it. Working as a reporter for the *New Orleans Item*, she interviewed the prizefighter Jack Dempsey and went undercover to report on the livelihood of the city's so-called taxi dancers. When informed that movie rights had been sold for her just-released novel, netting her an unexpected windfall, Dorothy returned to New York. There she bought a small beach cottage near other friends on Staten Island. Unbeknown to her, this place would become the locus of some of her richest joys and sorrows.

The little cottage off Arbutus Lake, overlooking Raritan Bay, is lovingly described by Dorothy in *The Long Loneliness*. Her happiness there—embodied in her love for Forster Batterham and their daughter Tamar Teresa, born in March 1926—remained forever life affirming. Suddenly Dorothy discovered not only the beauty of human fulfillment, but a consciousness that this was an entirely free gift and not of her making. This in turn unleashed an elemental sense of gratitude that turned her toward the only reality she thought could explain it: the source of all life and being itself. In a very real sense, Dorothy experienced unadulterated joy with Forster and Tamar on Staten Island, a characteristic sense she retained to the end of her days, including when life dealt her sorrow and separation, poverty and mistrust, blame, and a new sort of solitude. On Staten Island, she discovered that the natural and the supernatural were not two distinct realms. The natural often introduces the latter, after which life is forever altered. Somewhere, sometime, someplace, the beauty of a face, the touch of a hand, the expanse of a field, the color of light, or the revelation of a forest of constellations will leave one awestruck and acknowledging, if perhaps but for an instant, that there is more to life than what habitually occupies or addresses us.

The birth of her daughter, coupled with her love for Forster—before, during, and until the end of her life—proved to be Dorothy's "stargate," her breakthrough to wholeness. The effect was humanly expanding and created in her a deeper willingness to find God in the most unlikely of persons and situations.

When Forster could not come to terms with this new reality—he was not in favor of having Tamar baptized (for Dorothy, a crucial expression of her gratitude and her need to protect Tamar) or of having their own "marriage" solemnized (he accepted obedience to neither church nor state)—their days together were numbered. Dorothy did have Tamar christened that July and followed her into the Roman Catholic Church a year and a half later—not giving up on Forster until it was clear their positions on faith and marriage were unalterable and irreconcilable.

After that came five years in the desert for Dorothy. Many of her radical friends distanced themselves; Forster remained a sensual attraction, especially when he would visit; she had few Catholic friends, and those she did meet at the time, while devout, were not the sort to understand her plight or share her radical views. What ensued was single motherhood, another series of make-do jobs and moves, and the need to make sure Forster ponied up for Tamar's support—which he did. There was the loneliness and colorlessness of living amidst the Great Depression and the need to school herself in the catholicity of her newfound faith. The American Catholic Church was hardly a beacon of social or theological insight at the time. Still, she began writing for various Catholic journals, and this eventually led to a second break-through, meeting Peter Maurin in 1932. Thanks to George Shuster of *The Commonweal*, one of the journals she was writing for, Dorothy's introduction to Maurin permanently reset her life's trajectory. But in the five years prior to that, she and Tamar traveled widely—to Hollywood for Dorothy to pursue screen writing work, to Mexico, and finally back home to Florida and New York after Tamar had contracted malaria in Mexico.

In the fall of 1932, while sharing an apartment on East Fifteenth Street with her brother John and sister-in-law Tessa, Dorothy made a pilgrimage to the Shrine of the North American Martyrs in upstate New York. There she prayed for guidance. Nothing seemed to come of it immediately, but a few months later, she prayed again while on assignment to cover a series of demonstrations in Washington, DC. Franklin D. Roosevelt had just been elected president, but he would not be inaugurated until the following spring. Waves of marchers descended on Washington, calling for relief—for their farms, but also for those around their kitchen tables. The Communists were particularly active in organizing these rallies, and Dorothy admired their dedication and determination.

As a reporter, Dorothy stood on the periphery, a necessary observer. But this "distancing" only heightened her sense of noninvolvement and her new coreligionists' apparent lack of concern for the social situation. When she went to the National Shrine of the Immaculate Conception to pray again for discernment and direction, she was struck at how much more in sync she felt with the protest marchers than with her fellow Catholics. Nonetheless, she prayed—and she prayed well. (Of all the things Dorothy taught young people who came to the Catholic Worker, it was the seriousness of her approach to prayer. When you saw her at Mass, alone in church, or praying in her room, you knew what total attention meant.) As she explained, God takes you at your word. If you ask something, you'd better be ready to respond with your whole being. God's answer might come in a most unlikely guise—in Dorothy's case, the itinerant, street-corner preacher and philosopher Peter Maurin, twenty years her senior. He showed up at her apartment the day after she returned from Washington. Why she ever allowed him admittance, or more remarkable, offered it to him again, has to be a matter of how seriously she took her prayer.

Maurin convinced Dorothy that she was the one to start a paper that would relate Catholic social teaching (an almost "secret" body of wisdom, seldom preached from the pulpit even today) to Depression-era America. Maurin called for houses of hospitality to welcome the poor and the stranger, and for farming communes to put the unemployed back to work, what he called "the Green Revolution." The first issue of the *Catholic Worker* paper that they founded (May 1933) maxed out at twenty-five hundred copies, but within a year and a half, this tabloid-sized monthly had reached a circulation of one hundred thousand. As Tamar would later put it succinctly, "It just took off." The historian Mel Piehl has noted that the *Catholic Worker* was the first significant expression of Catholic radicalism in the United States. Dorothy and Peter, it seems, had roused a sleeping giant, and at a penny a copy nearly everyone who wanted an issue of the paper could afford it.

Soon other people began showing up at Dorothy's door and joining the cause. They were activists as well as journalists, and they started taking on the power brokers—on picket lines, in print, and in housing court. In 1934 these Catholic Workers demonstrated at the German consulate against the anti-Semitic laws of the new Hitler regime. The following year they protested Mussolini's invasion of Abyssinia—the movement and the paper's first foray into what would become the Catholic Worker's opposition to all wars. At the same time, people started showing up at the editorial office looking for food and shelter. At first hesitant, the staff soon felt compelled to respond, and thus evolved the movement's critical and perennial work of offering daily food, clothing, and hospitality to those in need.

Soon Dorothy was traveling the country to report for the paper and spread word of the Catholic Worker Movement's radical ideas of social reconstruction. In 1936 she incurred the wrath of the governor of Arkansas after she reported on the plight of tenant farmers in his state. He claimed she was a carpetbagger, a "Catholic woman" who, according to a Memphis newspaper, was making a fat salary "off the misery of the people."[1] That same year the *Catholic Worker* condemned the violence of both sides in the Spanish Civil War. This prophetic stance generated opposition from most mainline Catholics who supported Franco and his legions, and it led to a sharp drop in the paper's circulation. Still, the editors continued undaunted in their pacifist critique. A year later, Dorothy traveled to Flint, Michigan, to offer support for locked-out workers at the Fisher Body Plant. They raised her up through an open window and cheered her. The governor of Michigan invited her to talk. In 1939 she brought readers' attention to the racism she had met in two northern cities, Washington, DC, and Harrisburg, Pennsylvania. Later that year she made her first "Lacouture" retreat, which was inspired by a French-Canadian Jesuit who wished to apply the teaching of the gospels and the spirituality of St. Ignatius Loyola to the lives of twentieth-century people. For decades to come, the retreat was a hallmark of the Catholic Worker Movement. It deeply divided those who felt it was a rigorous but trustworthy means of spiritual growth and those who felt it bordered on a harsh, scrupulosity-inducing, and wrong-headed Jansenism.

In 1940 as the country readied for war, Dorothy testified before a congressional committee against reinstatement of conscription. The same year she wrote a commanding letter to all Catholic Worker affiliates, reminding them that pacifism was an integral, defining element of the movement, and that it would be better for those who, in conscience, could not adhere to this stance, to separate themselves voluntarily from the Catholic Worker. At the same time, she commended them and encouraged them to continue performing the works of mercy.

The day after Pearl Harbor, in a speech to the Liberal-Socialist Alliance in New York, she gave a ringing condemnation of all war. She called on men to resist the draft and women to resist false patriotism. She predicted that within a decade, weapons of mass destruction would be developed that would threaten human civilization. World War II, of course, changed everything immediately—in families, the country, and globally. Some Catholic Workers were drafted; others volunteered for the war. Some served time as conscientious objectors and as draft refusers. The staff of the paper dwindled, as did its circulation. Initially Dorothy had thought the paper might be suppressed by the government, but it was not.

Still, Dorothy decided to take a leave of absence in 1943–44, ostensibly to be near Tamar who was in school on Long Island, but also to be near her widowed mother, who was then living on Long Island. Dorothy retreated to a convent where she observed a self-imposed, semi-monastic regimen. But she realized soon enough, as she had in nursing school, that hers was a very different vocation: to journalism and the active life. She returned to the Catholic Worker in March 1944, and for the rest of the war she championed the paper's pacifist stance. Her editorial response to the dropping of atomic bombs on Hiroshima and Nagasaki remains a searing condemnation of all modern warfare. While Dorothy would later become discouraged by her continuing personal failures and those of the Catholic Worker Movement to achieve Peter Maurin's vision of "a new heaven and a new earth," her own vocation was never again in question. For the rest of her life her prayer was for faithfulness, constancy, and perseverance.

It was during and after World War II that the retreat movement, especially as preached by Fr. John Hugo of Pittsburgh, became an even more central thrust of the Catholic Worker. Dorothy wanted the movement's farms to serve not only as Peter Maurin's "agronomic universities," but also as retreat centers. She even wrote to Cardinal Francis Spellman of New York in 1946, asking for money to start a Catholic Worker retreat center on Staten Island—to no avail. In the decades to come, the Catholic Worker farms (at Easton, Pennsylvania;

Newburgh, New York; and later Staten Island and Tivoli, New York) all offered periodic retreats, until the late 1960s.

In 1949, Peter Maurin died after years of steady decline. Dorothy was thereafter the singular head of what many derided as a quixotic movement—admired for its service to the poor, but judged unrealistic when it came to war and social reconstruction. That same year Dorothy and others took on Cardinal Spellman for firing archdiocesan cemetery workers who were trying to form a union. Next came the Korean War, the anticommunism of the McCarthy and Cold War eras, and the nuclear arms race. At a communist-inspired rally at Carnegie Hall in 1952, Dorothy spoke against the Smith and McCarran Acts, but did so pointedly as a religious believer. She later deplored the tactics of Senator Joseph McCarthy, but faulted herself for having failed to maintain a sense of public respect for him. "There is no room for contempt of others in the Christian life," she wrote. "To criticize the social order is one thing, people another."[2] She herself was put on a watch list by the FBI's J. Edgar Hoover.

In 1952 Dorothy's *The Long Loneliness* was published. The following year a fire at the 223 Christie Street House in Manhattan resulted in the death of a resident. This led to Dorothy being declared a slum landlord, and she was fined by the court. The subsequent public outcry in her defense led to the judge rescinding his condemnation, but the Worker had to spend a huge sum to bring the house up to code. The poet W. H. Auden and others donated to the project, and it was completed, but only a few short years before the city condemned the property as part of a right-of-way order to build a new subway line. Finding new quarters for the soup line and the paper entailed years of expense and logistical strain. Several temporary moves resulted in added poverty and precariousness.

About this time, Ammon Hennacy joined the movement in New York. He had written for the paper for years and was a singular figure who never hesitated to describe himself as the "one-man revolution." He literally had nothing to do with the state and its war preparations, except when it came to repeatedly doing time in one of its jails for acts of civil disobedience. In 1955 he, Dorothy, and a small group began protesting New York City's annual mandatory nuclear defense drills, pointing out there would be no defense in the event of a nuclear attack. The group's willingness to go to jail, year after year, led to increasing numbers of demonstrators and a coalescing of public awareness concerning the futility of such exercises. Eventually the city terminated the drills in the early 1960s.

In 1954 as the French were facing defeat at Dien Bien Phu, Dorothy alerted *Catholic Worker* readers that it would be foolhardy for the United States to get involved in Vietnam. This proved another prophetic but unheeded warning. On the home front in 1957, while standing vigil at Koinonia Partners, an integrated community in Americus, Georgia, Dorothy was shot at from a speeding car. Flannery O'Connor commented drolly that it seemed a "long way to come to get shot at."[3] But in a short time, many others would head south to protest racial injustice, some of whom would pay the ultimate price to achieve equality and integration under the law. Dorothy told Ruth Collins that "no good work is ever achieved without blood," while acknowledging she had not yet "resisted unto blood" herself.

In 1958 and again in 1962, Dorothy traveled to Mexico, the latter time following a month-long reporting trip to Cuba. This Cuban trip was one of the most controversial of her career. Her positive dispatches about day-to-day life under Castro were uncommon for an American journalist.

But they were soon overshadowed by the geopolitical nuclear crisis that erupted weeks after her return.

The following spring, women activists from around the world, including Dorothy, made a pilgrimage to Rome to pray for peace. Pope John XXIII's *Pacem in Terris* had just been issued, and during his final public appearance he seems to have singled out these peace pilgrims. Dorothy returned to Rome again in 1965 for the final session of the Second Vatican Council. While there, she fasted and prayed for a strong conciliar condemnation of nuclear warfare and for the right of individuals to declare conscientious objection to wars. The council affirmed both of these positions.

When Dorothy returned to New York in November 1965, she was again thrown into the crucible. Almost immediately she was involved in an antiwar demonstration supporting young men who burned their selective service cards, among them several Catholic Workers. A few days later, Roger La-Porte, a young volunteer who had been associated briefly with the Catholic Worker and had attended the draft card rally, immolated himself outside United Nations headquarters. He did so, he said, in the hope of ending all wars. When he died two days later, Dorothy was blamed by some for the tragedy. She reached out to LaPorte's family and wrote movingly in her column about his misguided act. But she also wrote about how the young Catholic Workers had cared for LaPorte, and she concluded by drawing her readers' attention to the forgiving mercy of God.

In 1967 Dorothy returned to Rome. She was chosen to represent Americans at the Third World Congress on the Lay Apostolate and to receive Communion from Pope Paul VI. While in Italy she interviewed Ignazio Silone and visited Danilo Dolci, the Gandhi of Sicily. In 1970 she traveled around the world, touching down in Hong Kong before traveling on to India, Australia, Tanzania, and England. The following year she journeyed to Poland, Bulgaria, Hungary, and the Soviet Union. When she criticized a group of Soviet writers in Moscow for their failure to defend Alexander Solzhenitsyn, they got up and walked out. In 1973 she traveled to England and to Ireland.

The year before, the Nixon administration had threatened to close down the Catholic Worker, saying it had failed to pay income taxes totaling hundreds of thousands of dollars for the previous six years. After a public outcry, the government retreated; after all, there were no salaries to be taxed at the Catholic Worker. As Dorothy wrote in the paper at the time, "To resist is to survive."

In the 1960s Dorothy traveled multiple times across the United States to the West Coast. There she reported on Cesar Chavez and his United Farm Workers movement. When she visited again in 1973, she was arrested and jailed for the final time. On August 6, 1976, the anniversary of the dropping of the bomb on Hiroshima, she spoke before the International Eucharistic Congress in Philadelphia. There she called on the church and the nation to do penance for unleashing the bomb and for our country's continued wars and preparation for war. Not long afterwards, she suffered several heart attacks. In 1980 she was hospitalized for heart failure, but demanded that she be brought home to Maryhouse. She died there in the company of her daughter on November 29. It was the eve of Advent, and Dorothy had just turned eighty-three.

CHAPTER TWO

Radical Roots, Molecular Moral Forces

The sketchy itinerary of Dorothy's life in the previous chapter provides little more than a Monday-morning box score. A person's life cannot be measured in miles or years or even achievements. Dorothy would agree. Life is to be understood and judged on how one lives each day, each moment.

That is certainly what mattered most to those who actually lived and worked with Dorothy: her sense of presence among them and her willingness to listen; her attention to the moment; her ability to put everything—wild and tame, broad and simple, political and spiritual—in a context of purpose and eternity. As Elie Wiesel described the Baal Shem Tov (1700–1760), the founder of Hasidism: "He considered it an art of virtue to listen to others." And again, "I can still hear my grandfather telling me: 'In the Besht's universe, no one felt left out.' "[1]

Notwithstanding her stature, perhaps even her renown, there was a shyness about Dorothy one did not expect.

Generally she did not like to have her picture taken, and most acquaintances refrained from doing so in deference to her unwritten request. In many snapshots of her, she seems to be looking down or to the side. Even when looking directly at a photographer, as in some early group portraits with other Catholic Workers, she seems uneasy. Later, this was not always the case, especially when Stanley Vishnewski, who came to the Catholic Worker in 1934 and remained until his death forty-five years later, was prowling about, nonchalantly snapping pictures and telling tall tales while entertaining whomever happened to be around. Nor was it always the case when professional photographers were at work. For Bob Fitch, Richard Avedon, Jon Erikson, Vivian Cherry, and Bill Barrett, for example, there were direct gazes. But even for the likes of Berenice Abbot and Ed Lettau, the eyes could be looking down or off to the side.

But Dorothy's gaze was not that way when she was with individuals. Then a sense of direct address prevailed. Yet, in groups or when people pressed in on her, her rudimentary modesty seemed to come to the fore, creating a protective space. People would still crowd around, introduce themselves, and start sharing their stories. And if someone like me happened to be standing nearby, she would pull the person forward and introduce that person—as if he or she was the one whom people had come out to see that evening.

Others found Dorothy's eyes unsettling. In Nicole d'Entremont's novel *City of Belief*, which deals with the dramatic events of the Roger LaPorte tragedy, the Dorothy character is described by the young narrator as having the eyes of a rattler. Columnist Nicholas von Hoffman reported he had met Dorothy only once ("when she was an old lady"), but that she had "the fast, fierce eye of an eagle. It gleamed and it was quick."[2] Indeed, Dorothy was quick—

and she was no reporter's fool. Garry Wills told *Esquire* readers in 1983 that she had "Modigliani eyes."[3] Modigliani himself might have been charmed—as were others. Some scholars speculate that Eugene O'Neill's Josie in *Moon for the Misbegotten* was inspired, in part, by Dorothy.

One can learn a great deal about Dorothy from her friendships, from the people who visited her through the years, and also from those who wanted to write for her or to speak at the Catholic Worker. Early on Jacques Maritain, the philosopher and later diplomat, came to visit, as did Sigrid Undset, the Nobel Prize-winning Norwegian author who was forced to flee her homeland by the Nazis. There were poets and authors: W. H. Auden, Hilaire Belloc, J. F. Powers, and Dwight Macdonald. There was the cultural historian Lewis Mumford and reporters like Mike Wallace and Bill Moyers. There were radicals Bayard Rustin, A. J. Muste, and Dave Dellinger; union leaders John L. Lewis and Cesar Chavez; and psychologists and psychiatrists Karl Stern, Erik Erikson, and Robert Coles. The philosopher Hannah Arendt came to speak, and the poet Allen Ginsberg to recite. Rabbi Abraham Joshua Heschel invited her to his home, as did Mother Teresa and her sisters in Calcutta. There was Joan Baez and the jazz composer Mary Lou Williams. Thomas Merton wrote for the paper, as did the Berrigan brothers. Frank Sheed, Maisie Ward, and their son Wilfrid Sheed were longstanding friends. The list would fill pages.

Besides the radicals, the literati, the artists, and the theologians, there were the sisters and priests, politicians and ecumenists, publishers and news reporters, and *always* the down and outs and the troubled. Once the Catholic Worker got started, the poor were always with her—Mr. Breen, Smokey Joe, Farmer John, Smitty, Italian Mike, Russian Mike, Ukrainian Mike, Polish Mike, Polish Walter, Scottie,

Darwin, Slim, Missouri Marie, Hans, Scottish Mary, Earl, Tobey, Julia, Mad Paul, Millie, John the Baptist, Jimmy, Anna, Sr. Jeanette, Eleanor, Whiskers, Wong—the names form a litany of sinners and saints, some of whom you might not wish to see again until Judgment Day. Yet all of them found in Dorothy a North Star, a light in August.

Dorothy could inspire uneasiness among the settled and the accomplished—those whose lives were largely spent in safety and who traveled on level roads. She could make some people uncomfortable simply by sitting near them in her hand-me-down clothes or by saying matter-of-factly that the church should sell the bulk of its property and give the proceeds to the poor. Five years after her death, William F. Buckley Jr. told his *National Review* audience that he doubted "99 percent of Americans remembered the name Dorothy Day," whom he called "the saintly ascetic who was careless enough to confuse Christianity and socialism."[4] In 1972 Dorothy told a young Jesuit that his group's work in the social order had been tremendously important in the past, when members of his community were concerned with "more fundamental things than they do now when they're dealing in politics." Her radical approach had not only to do with her personality or her ideals, but also with her experience and her analysis of what would make for a better society—for everyone, including the rich.

Before her conversion, Dorothy had been inspired by the homegrown socialism of Eugene V. Debs and the decentralist philosophy of the Industrial Workers of the World, particularly their sense of solidarity and responsibility for one another, their selflessness, and long-term goals. She contrasted these with what she saw every day in the slums where she lived: "The stink of the world's injustice and the world's indifference is all around us," she said.

From her earliest years—and this is part of her quintessential Americanness—Dorothy was taken with the notion of human freedom and the inviolability of conscience. They are major themes in her writing and were issues eventually incorporated into official Catholic teaching itself at the Second Vatican Council. In July 1965, more than thirty years after the start of the Catholic Worker Movement, Dorothy wrote that freedom is "God's greatest gift to man." In December that same year, the council would promulgate *Dignitatis Humanae*, its "Declaration on Religious Freedom." (It was later called "one of the major texts" of the council by Pope Paul VI.) While she was fasting in Rome during the final session of the council, Dorothy took note of the declaration's prime advocate, American Jesuit John Courtney Murray, writing his name in large red letters in her diary.

For Dorothy, freedom could not be separated from the notion of personal responsibility and care for the common good. In a list of what the Catholic Worker stood for, compiled and jotted down by a young resident at the Tivoli farm, Dorothy was happy to find the following: "Seeing Christ in each person; nonviolence; voluntary poverty; the works of mercy." But then she added, "You forgot one thing: Freedom!" Charles Péguy, the French Catholic poet who died in the trenches in 1914, reminded his contemporaries that freedom was God's gift and creation, and that salvation itself had to be freely chosen. For, he asked, "What kind of salvation would a salvation be that was not free?" Aligned with this imperative for human freedom came personal respect for—and acceptance of and care for—others and the common good. As Péguy has God inquire elsewhere of those arriving at heaven's gate: "And where are the others?"[5]

This notion of personal freedom/responsibility, coupled with acceptance of others and the inclusivity of the common good, has led Catholic Workers to repeatedly practice Henry David Thoreau's American-style civil disobedience. In 1952 Dorothy told readers, "The Catholic Worker's respect for freedom has meant our opposition to the draft, to buying war bonds, and to the paying of taxes." These actions, some punishable by law, demanded a personal, and sometimes exacting, decision. Like Thoreau, Peter Maurin believed that law, good or bad, could never make people good. In fact, Maurin felt, the law had deteriorated into a system to protect property values and the profit system. As a result, Dorothy said, there was nothing Maurin was more averse to than the state, "the all-encroaching state."

The French political thinker Pierre Proudhon had written in 1864 that anarchism "is a form of government or constitution" in which the principles of authority—including police institutions, bureaucracy, taxation, etc.—"are reduced to their simplest terms."[6] Such a view of anarchism, while far from the common understanding that allies it with lawlessness and mayhem, is close to what Maurin was agitating for. Asked directly (and repeatedly) about the Catholic Worker's use of the term, Dorothy responded in an October 1957 appeal letter that, "those dread words, pacifism and anarchism—when you get right down to it—mean that we try always to love rather than coerce, 'to be what we want the other fellow to be,' to be the least, to have no authority over others, to begin . . . with ourselves."

Judith Gregory, who knew Dorothy for decades—before and after working at the CW in the late 1950s and early '60s—said that Dorothy's genius was "not to close out anything." That's why Dorothy would repeatedly surprise you. George P. Carlin, who was around the Worker in the late 1940s and eventually was ordained a priest in the Philippines, described Dorothy as "paradoxical to those trying to typecast her." He told of a conversation in the late '60s when, to his surprise, she was "boasting like a doting grandmother" about her grandson Eric, who was serving in Vietnam. "I was popeyed," said Carlin. "I said to myself, 'I can't believe what I'm hearing, Dorothy the pacifist.' "[7] But, he continued, *that* was Dorothy: "She had her own strong beliefs. But all she asked of anyone else was to reflect and then act on one's conscience. Once the person had decided, Dorothy was the first to totally respect the decision, even if it was one hundred eighty degrees away from her own personal conclusions."

At the start of World War II when Tom Sullivan, a Chicago Catholic Worker, enlisted in the army, Dorothy tried to dissuade him: Why didn't he become a conscientious objector, like other Catholic Workers? "Because," Tom told her, alluding to Hitler, "I think the bastard is trying to kill us." Sullivan was posted to the Pacific and remained there for the duration. Dorothy wrote to him throughout the war, and when he was discharged, he came for a visit in New York. Dorothy welcomed him and even encouraged him to rejoin the movement. They had been talking together in the soup kitchen when she said to him cheekily, "Why don't you go over there and start doing the dishes?" Not to be cowed, Sullivan responded, "I'll do the washing if you do the drying." She got up, grabbed a dishtowel, and Sullivan stayed to become a mainstay of the movement—managing the house, the bank account, and the paper for ten years—before eventually leaving to join the Trappists.

"There is always a great need for idealists," Dorothy said early in the movement's history, people "who uphold the ideal rather than the practical. Without them men would not strive so high. Little by little, it can be found that the ideal works and is practical, and then men are surprised." The Catholic Worker surprised many over the years, including one historian who recently described it as the longest enduring experiment in the history of American radicalism. In part, it has endured because it has endeavored to stay small. "God forbid we should have great institutions," Dorothy told Jeff Dietrich of the Los Angeles Catholic Worker in 1971. "The thing is to have many small centers. The ideal is community."

One of Dorothy's favorite quotations, repeated often and reprinted in the paper and on thank-you cards, is a testament of William James: "I am done with great things and big things, great institutions and big success, and I am for those invisible, molecular moral forces that work from individual to individual, creeping through the crannies of the world like so many rootlets . . . which, if you give them time, will rend the hardest monuments of man's pride."[8]

Dorothy Day's radical conviction, buttressed further by her conversion, was that we are all made in the image and likeness of God, and that as a result we have an infinite purpose and destiny.

CHAPTER THREE

Conversions

It is impossible to separate the preconversion, radical Dorothy Day from the woman who, by the time of her death, had prophetically, albeit incrementally, altered the consciousness of the American Catholic Church.

Unlike some neophytes, when Dorothy converted to Catholicism she seemed to have embraced its full range and depth. This is not to imply there was ever a sense she was trying to make up for lost years or trying to be "more Catholic" than others. Rather, by the time I came to know her she simply seemed to be the complete package: an incomparable instructor in church history, practice, devotion, and lore. Her instruction was given not in a formal classroom but imparted around the kitchen table, during conversations in the office or in her room, or while walking slowly to Mass. In all these venues she would discuss what she had just read, recommend a book, or send her listeners on assignment: to union halls, a conference center, or a nursing home. And she would tell stories, stories that seemed to well up without end (you can get a sense of this by reading her selected diaries). These were engrossing and served as an in-depth instruction for new Catholic Workers like me.

Dorothy would remark that she had been a Socialist in college and a Communist for a while, but that their class–war approach had left her cold. She felt human solidarity was the key to real and enduring revolution. Here you can pick up strains of Peter Kropotkin and his criticism of Darwin and Herbert Spencer's survival-of-the-fittest paradigm. For Kropotkin, the key to evolution was cooperation rather than competition or "creative destruction." "Radicalism had a great deal to do with my conversion," Dorothy told Dean Brackley, a young Jesuit, in 1972, but her own conversion, she continued, had more to do with "reading books on the spiritual life."

Those books were far ranging and perhaps sometimes far afield. She told Thomas Merton that Dostoyevsky was spiritual reading for her. She said Joris–Karl Huysmans's *The Cathedral*, given her by a Communist friend, had opened Catholicism to her in an unanticipated way. She gave Kathleen and me an Edmund Wilson essay on *Doctor Zhivago* because, she said, she found it such a profound reflection on the resurrection. One of her preconversion "a-ha" moments had been reading William James's reflection on the radical freedom afforded by voluntary poverty. "We have grown literally afraid to be poor," he lamented. "We despise anyone who elects to be poor in order to save his inner life. If he does not join the general scramble, we deem him spiritless and lacking in ambition." According to James, Americans had lost the power to even imagine what "the ancient realization of poverty could have meant: the liberation from material attachments, the unbribed soul."[1]

The unbribed—freed—soul was what Dorothy was after. Following her conversion this would include learning to place absolute trust in God. First, that meant waiting for God to show her a way (Peter Maurin). Then, for the rest of her days, it meant trusting in God to provide for the myriad needs of the Catholic Worker adventure.

It is helpful to reconsider what was involved in Dorothy's conversion. It was a veritable tsunami that resulted from her daughter's birth. "She was, of course, everything to me," Dorothy wrote of Tamar in 1952. "I have not even to this day ceased to look upon her with wonder."[2]

Still, before that there were intimations of wonder in many of Dorothy's experiences (some recorded in *The Long Loneliness*). As a girl she had seen others at prayer, and it had impressed her immensely. In Greenwich Village, in the company of Gene O'Neill, she had fled the "hound of heaven" down labyrinthine ways. In solitary confinement outside Washington, DC, she had rediscovered the solace of the psalms. Then there was reading Victor Hugo in Paris and, following her failed marriage, being given and reading Huysmans in Chicago. At that same time she had been impressed with the chaste lives of several Catholic women her age with whom she was rooming. There had been the abiding goodness of her lone Catholic aunt. Finally there was some mysterious, embracing sense she encountered when she first read the Bible as a child, and later when she stepped into churches in lower Manhattan and watched as immigrants and workers unselfconsciously went on with their prayers. The odors of those churches appealed to her, as did the candles and the stained glass. One of the things that impressed Dorothy about the church, she related, was that it took into account body and soul, all the senses. Even "telling your beads" was part of that, for such things appeal to the senses, and it is through the senses that we learn. As the Irish poet Patrick Kavanagh put it, "God is in the bits and pieces of Everyday. . . . A pearl necklace round the neck of poverty."[3]

Dorothy's breakup with Forster was without question the most immediate, searing, and long-lasting test of her new faith. First there was the bald aloneness that ensued, the sheer absence of touch. She missed him body and soul, and by the end of their time together, she had to literally kick him out and bar the door. Then there was the new practicality: how to provide for Tamar? And, must one—a single mother—have to repeatedly importune the absent father? ("To importune" was one of Dorothy's signature phrases. People were always importuning her, she said: to print their articles—especially their *long* ones—to have her spend more time with *them*, to support *their* dubious causes and battles, etc., etc.) Then there was her guilt for having "broken up" the family. She would confess, even decades later, how unjust she was to have separated Tamar from her father—how unaware of their pain she was at the time. "Forgive us our unknown faults," Dorothy used to say, and pray. She was already quite aware of her *known* faults.

"My Catholicism was an act of faith," Dorothy wrote in *Commonweal* in 1958. "It had seemed like death at the time, to become a Catholic."[4] But she took sustenance in the words of Scripture: "Though He slay me, yet will I trust Him." And slay her God seemed intent on doing: "For me, Christ was not bought for thirty pieces of silver," she told readers in 1967, "but with my heart's blood. We buy not cheap in this market."[5]

Faith, according to New Testament scholar Luke Timothy Johnson, is "the complete response of human freedom to God, involving trust, obedience, and endurance."[6] Dorothy developed trust, obedience, and endurance by working at it 24-7 from week to week and year to year. "Each act of faith," she would say, "increases your faith." She would say it matter-of-factly. And if it happened to be a particularly harrowing time at the First Street House, she would add, again matter-of-factly (but with a note of encouragement), "Pray and endure." These and other Pauline-like phrases seemed to be on the tip of her tongue, and to spring from a level of consciousness just beneath whatever else she might be talking about.

One of the ancient Irish prayers begins by invoking "the power of faith." Faith is a relationship (trust) that becomes second nature—as in a true marriage or friendship—by being practiced and nurtured. For Dorothy, the power of faith was recalibrated, recharged, and redeployed daily in her work and prayer. For she had to ask God, without ceasing, to expand the walls (of the house and of her heart), to deepen the soup pot, to send new workers, to pay the baker for his rock-hard bread and the printer—who demanded "pay and pray" (at least *he* had a sense of humor).

Her long search and having had to give up "human love when it was dearest and tenderest," were as confounding to Dorothy as to old friends, and even new ones. Yet as she later reflected in *The Long Loneliness*, "I wanted life and I wanted abundant life. I wanted it for others, too. I wanted a synthesis. . . . I wanted everyone to be kind . . . every home to be open to the lame, the halt, and the blind." Only then, she wrote, would people really live, really love one another. In such love, she thought, was the abundant life. But prior to her conversion, and for the first five years following it, she said she "did not have the slightest idea how to find it."

By temperament Dorothy was independent, strong willed, and a self-starter. When she asked to be shown a way, she also went out of *her* way to find it. She started studying her new faith and writing for Catholic publications. (To pay the rent, Dorothy wrote not only for Catholic journals but for some of her old radical ones.) One summer on Staten Island, she worked at a nearby Marist novitiate, imbibing its culture while attending to her duties. She came to understand the life of a religious community, as Robert Browning had done in his 1842 dramatic monologue "Soliloquy in a Spanish Cloister." She used these insights for her short story "The Brother and the Rooster," published in *Commonweal*.[7] She also began what would become a lifelong commitment to reading the lives of the saints, in multiple collections and editions. She didn't find these heroines and heroes spineless, pious wimps, but rather rebels with a cause. Nonetheless, she often quoted one of her spiritual directors that one must beware of slavish imitation: "One could go to hell imitating the imperfections of the saints." Through her reading she discovered how these unique individuals addressed the exigencies of their times—poverty, the struggle for power (spiritual and temporal), and pride, pride, pride—and that they knew a great deal about both eros and agape.

In September 1932 on her pilgrimage to Auriesville, she read and liked a book about the Jesuits that her old friend, Edna Kenton—they had shared an apartment one summer in Greenwich Village—had written. Her prayers in upstate New York and later in Washington, led, Dorothy was sure, to her subsequent encounter with Peter Maurin.

This encounter might be called a "second conversion." Like Christ's disciples, Dorothy not only threw in her nets at the Lord's command, she left everything to follow him. And once that happens, once one is united in Christ, a new world has begun. As Paul wrote to the Corinthians (2 Cor 5:17), "there is a new creation: everything old has passed away; see, everything has become new!"

Peter Maurin certainly wanted such a new world order. Dubbed "an apostle on the bum" by Dwight Macdonald in the *New Yorker*,[8] Peter had emigrated from France to Canada in 1909 and a few years later to the United States. He was a reader and a rover. John Moody of the Wall Street investment firm called him one of the smartest men he ever met. Dorothy would later write that Peter was the holiest man she ever met. These two remarkable qualities—intelligence and holiness—however, arrived at Dorothy's door in the most unlikely packaging: a middle-aged, Depression-era man from the street.

Peter Maurin spoke with a strong French accent (his family could trace its roots back centuries in Languedoc, southern France), and, perhaps emulating the staccato poetry of Charles Péguy, Peter expressed himself in short, pithy sentences and essays, so distilled that on first reading they struck many as simplistic. "What we give to the poor for Christ's sake is what we carry with us when we die," he wrote.[9] Distilled—and sobering.

Maurin was so steeped in Catholicism and the history of Christendom that the so-called age of faith seemed his natural frame of reference. Dorothy, on the other hand, brought an added and necessary breadth to their collaboration that included her American experience and a convert's background. Peter wanted to return not simply to a pre-industrialized era or to medieval monasticism, but all the way back to first-century Christianity. In a certain sense, Peter wanted to go back to go forward, whereas Dorothy wanted to go forward to go back.

The Catholic Worker's foundation was set entirely on two pillars, which can be found in the Gospel of Matthew: the Sermon on the Mount (chapters 5 and 6) and Jesus' criteria for entering eternal life (chapter 25). From these two great plinths spring all the Catholic Worker has preached and practiced—the corporal and spiritual works of mercy, the works of peace and justice, the path of active nonviolence, dying to oneself, the forgiveness of enemies, the primacy of love, and purity of heart. Peter compressed them into one of his poem/essays "What Makes Man Human":

> To give and not to take,
> that is what makes [us] human.
> To serve and not to rule,
> that is what makes [us] human.
> To help and not to crush,
> that is what makes [us] human.
> To nourish and not to destroy,
> that is what makes [us] human.
> And if need be, to die and not to live,
> that is what makes [us] human.[10]

This short poem/essay establishes Peter's bottom line, his cultural analysis of the modern era, and what we ought to do to redeem our present situation. His "At a Sacrifice" furthers this analysis:

> In the first centuries of Christianity
> the hungry were fed
> at a personal sacrifice,
> the naked were clothed
> at a personal sacrifice,
> the homeless were sheltered
> at a personal sacrifice.
> And because the poor were fed, clothed, and sheltered
> at a personal sacrifice,
> the pagans used to say about the Christians,
> "See how they love each other."
>
> In our own day
> the poor are no longer
> fed, clothed, and sheltered

at a personal sacrifice,
but at the expense of the taxpayer.
And because the poor are no longer
fed, clothed, and sheltered,
the pagans say about the Christians,
"See how they pass the buck."[11]

When Peter Maurin arrived at Dorothy's apartment on East Fifteenth Street in December 1932, she noticed that the pockets in his tattered overcoat were bulging with papers. They turned out to be the writings of two people she was both familiar with and valued: Kropotkin and St. Francis of Assisi. Learned as Peter was, radical as he was, and poor like Francis as he was, he often carried what he had of a "library" entirely in his pockets or in his head. The confluence of the two thinkers he brought with him that first meeting bore real significance for Dorothy and alerted her to the primacy the two played in Peter's worldview, its social as well as its spiritual aspects.

As previously mentioned, Kropotkin was an anarchist whose aim was to create a peaceful, cooperative society based on assuming personal responsibility for one's life and one's community, rather than relinquishing that job to the state. Maurin preferred the appellation "personalist communitarian" to "anarchist." What he was looking for—and, from others' testimony, what he embodied—is outlined in any number of his poems/essays. Here is his definition of "The Personalist Communitarian":

A personalist
is a go-giver
not a go-getter.
He tries to give
what he has

and does not
try to get
what the other fellow has.
He tries to be good
by doing good
to the other fellow.
He is altro-centered,
not self-centered.
He has a social doctrine
of the common good.
He spreads the social doctrine
of the common good
through words and deeds.
He speaks through deeds
as well as words, for he knows that deeds
speak louder than words.
Through words and deeds
he brings into existence
a common unity
the common unity
of a community.[12]

For Maurin, labor (work) was not a commodity—something to be bought and sold—but the individual's means of self-expression and a gift to the common good. In contrast to what he called an acquisitive society—detailed in the writings of British economist R. H. Tawney—Peter called for a functional society, one in which each member strives to contribute to and foster the common good: "a society of go-givers instead of go-getters; a society of idealists rather than materialists." This philosophy was "so old it seemed like new," Peter would remark. In fact, as the Italian priest Dom Luigi Sturzo, exiled by Mussolini, wrote in his 1939 book *Church and State*, "The early Christians represented a new associative force, which expanded from religion to the political plane; their anarchy was not antisocial but truly social; their action was . . . constructive."[13]

Twenty years after Peter's death, Dorothy remarked on "the terrible simplicity of these ideals" and how halting had been the Catholic Worker's own realization, let alone achievement, of them. But it was not as if Peter's vision hadn't achieved some results. His three-pronged emphasis—on houses of hospitality (where the works of mercy would be practiced daily "at a personal cost"), a newspaper and discussion groups for the clarification of thought, and farming communes that would allow people to pursue meaningful work while providing for their needs and those of others— was and continues to be the critical vision of Catholic Worker communities around the world.

Peter Maurin put a great emphasis on the need for physical work. Dorothy once told me that the two men she admired most were Peter Maurin and Ammon Hennacy. Her reason, however, surprised me. It was not because she valued Peter for his synthesis or Hennacy for his activism, but because both were extraordinary hands-on workers. Besides his writing and conversing, Peter would do demanding physical jobs each day. Hennacy, who spent a life at hard labor along with demonstrating against war and serving time in prison, would religiously spend the first part of his day at the Catholic Worker assisting in the work of the house and the paper. Ida Görres, in her study of the life of St. Thérèse of Lisieux, observed that "the one inexhaustible school of mortification is work." As Thérèse came to embody her "little way," every ordinary task of the day was to be done precisely, attending to "the one thing indisputably important here and now, without let or pause, and at all costs."[14] This little way of St. Thérèse became for Dorothy a spirituality for our times.

Like Fr. Zosima in *The Brothers Karamazov*, Peter Maurin saw the supreme value of work in its communitarian aspect. Each person's work, to quote Zosima, "contributes to the salvation of the whole world." These were also Benedictine ideas, where work and prayer join to become a seamless unity. As Dorothy wrote in 1933, "We want more than a weekly wage. We want God to teach us love."

Finally, physical work was important for Peter because it engaged both body and soul. He felt there would be far fewer nervous breakdowns "if men worked with their hands, instead of just their heads." And work was elemental because it mirrored the divine action, creating a sense of self-fulfillment, wonder, and self-emptying love to serve the common good.

Maurin's call for "work, not wages" fell flat on Depression-era ears. As Dorothy remarked years later, but before Peter's death, "Peter Maurin believes in the technique of surprise. He thinks people need to be startled. But I wonder sometimes if we don't startle them too much."[15] Her calls for the right of workers to organize, to demand a living wage, and to rewrite current legislation outlawing such things as child labor, were all in sync with the tenor of Catholic social teaching. And while she agreed with Peter's critique that unions had settled for wage concessions rather than demanding a share in ownership (and the responsibility that goes with it), she knew that men and women did not live on work alone, and that improving one's lot depends on simultaneously improving the lot of others.

Until the end of her life, Dorothy Day called Peter Maurin her mentor and teacher. Without him, we might never have become aware of her. His teaching was a forerunner of what in 2005 the *Compendium of the Social Doctrine of the Church* described as "a humanism capable of creating a new social, economic, and political order founded on the dignity and freedom of every human person."[16] As Dorothy and Peter put it, but in fewer words, what they wanted and were working for was "a society where it would be easier for people to be good."

CHAPTER FOUR

Principles and Convergences

In response to people asking how to start a Catholic Worker paper, farm, or house of hospitality, Dorothy would say simply, "The most important thing is just to get started." She would then offer encouragement to the beginners, telling them just how *exciting* "getting started" was. It seemed as if she were experiencing again the vitality she felt during the first years of the Catholic Worker.

In part this was because Dorothy was still living the life, and it was (is) never dull. The excitement and engagement were never something in the past for her. Rather, it was her daily, ongoing experience, and each day brought with it unique challenges, surprises, and beginnings.

I remember sitting in the paper room (the second-floor space where the paper was edited, the addresses were run off, and the ninety-thousand copies were folded by hand, labeled, and put in canvas bags for delivery to the post office) with two vice presidents from the IBM corporation. They had requested a meeting because IBM was unhappy it was being leafleted down on Wall Street for its role in the Vietnam War. The leafleting came from several young, articulate

Catholic Workers at the time. Dorothy approved of their action—both their initiative and how they had gone about it. Like so many things that happen at the Catholic Worker, this particular effort grew up almost spontaneously, thanks not to Dorothy but to the insight and work of others. Even though she didn't say a word at the meeting, her presence encouraged those who were leading the protest.

Years before, Dorothy had written, "We were the first Catholics to picket the Mexican and German embassies, to protest the persecution of the church in Mexico and the persecution of Jews and Catholics in Germany." She was referring to the mid-1930s, when the Worker had spontaneously and nearly single-handedly made those protests. And, she added, "We have picketed the Russian consulate, and have consistently pointed out our fundamental opposition to atheistic communism."[1] When it came to making such protests, how many Americans had the slightest idea of what was happening in Mexico or Germany at the time, or, for that matter, IBM's role in the Vietnam War? In 1957 during the frenzy of the Cold War, Dorothy wrote, "We were setting our faces against the world, against things as they are, the terrible injustice of our capitalist industrial system which lives by war and by preparation for war."[2] That same year she pointed out, in a leaflet calling for people to resist participating in civil defense drills, "We love our country and are only saddened to see its great virtues matched by equally great faults. We are part of it, we are responsible too."

The Catholic Worker opposed all materialisms—militant communism as well as bloody-fanged capitalism. Living among the poor meant that Catholic Workers daily witnessed and experienced the inequities and injustices of the US economic system: "The class structure is of *our* making and by our consent," Dorothy wrote in 1953—not God's—"and we must do what we can to change it. So we are urging revolutionary change."[3] Five years earlier she had written, "We are not expecting utopia here on earth. But God meant for things to be made easier than we have made them."[4]

Even during World War II, Dorothy and the CW kept up this approach. She wrote in her 1948 diary: "The present vast possessions of the Robber Barons need to be overthrown, cast down, appropriated, decentralized, distributed, etc. A vast reform is needed. The power of the corporations . . . the great banks will be overthrown, and that is something to be looked forward to."[5] For Dorothy, it would be the same story and the same indictment today. That is why, as she wrote in her column the same year, "We must resist, we must change by nonviolent means, an iniquitous social order that leads to war."[6] For her, the problem was not that idealism had failed, but that imagination and will had. In *The Long Loneliness* she famously questioned why so much energy was put into remedying social evils that could have been avoided in the first place: "Where were the saints to try to change the social order," she asked, "not just to minister to slaves but to do away with slavery?"[7]

The source of the radicality of the Catholic Worker, and of Dorothy, are found in the life and teachings of Jesus (Luke 6:27–30): "But I say to you that listen, Love your enemies, do good to those who hate you, bless those who curse you, pray for those who abuse you. If anyone strikes you on the cheek, offer the other also; and from anyone who takes away your coat do not withhold even your shirt. Give to everyone who begs from you; and if anyone takes away your goods, do not ask for them again." And then the clincher (6:35): "Love your enemies, do good, and lend, expecting nothing in return. Your reward will be great, and you will be children of the Most High."

Dorothy had observed in her 1944 diary that it was impossible, "save by heroic charity, to live in the present social order and be Christians." By "charity" she did not mean simply, or principally, almsgiving—although this is a permanent obligation—but the theological virtue of love for God and one's neighbor, a love so complete it could forgive wrongs, embrace one's foes, and change one's lifestyle.

Dom Helder Camara, the archbishop of Recife, Brazil, recounted that when he was very young, he thought Christ exaggerated about the dangers wealth occasions. "Now," as an older person, Camara reflected, "I know that it is extraordinarily difficult to combine wealth and human sensitivity."[8] The life of shared poverty allowed Dorothy and the Catholic Workers not only to understand the poor but to write about poverty from a living, personal perspective. This meant she was not simply speculating about poverty but seeing the world through its reality. Sometimes she accomplished this with an irony that could be caustic. "I find a little paragraph in my notebook," she wrote in the April 1934 *Catholic Worker*:

> Michael Norton, porter, idle for five years, brought in $2. It was a thanksgiving offering, he explained, and he wanted to give it to some of our children in honor of his daughter in Ireland.

> And I remember how I spoke down in Palm Beach last month before the Four Arts Club, on the invitation of a convert. They told me, when I had finished, "You know we never pay speakers," and another woman said, with a tremor, "Miss Day, I hope you can convey to your readers and listeners that we would give our very souls to help the poor, if we saw any constructive way of doing it." And still another told me, "The workers come to my husband's mill and beg him with tears in their eyes to save them from

unions. I hope you don't mind me saying so, but I think you are all wrong when it comes to unions."

They were all deeply moved, they told me, by the picture of conditions in Arkansas and the steel districts and the coal-mining districts, but: "You can't do anything with them, you know, these poor people. It seems to me the best remedy is birth control and sterilization."

We are told to keep a just attitude toward the rich, and we try. But as I thought of our breakfast line, our crowded house with people sleeping on the floor, when I thought of cold tenement apartments around us, and the lean, gaunt faces of the men who come to us for help, desperation in their eyes, it was impossible not to hate, with a hearty hatred and with a stronger anger, the injustice of this world.

This "hearty hatred," it must be noted, was directed not against individuals but against a system that creates and maintains widespread, profound disparities and injustice. Dorothy had a Faulkner-like understanding of the strata of the individual human heart and of how each one of us is unknowingly affected by the social milieu of which we are a part.

"Peter Maurin says it is the duty of the journalist to make history as well as record it," Dorothy wrote in 1939.[9] A decade later, in an article titled "The Scandal of the Works of Mercy" for *Commonweal*, she observed that despite all the work that goes on in academic conferences, classrooms, and even in periodical articles, "much of it comes to words, and not very vital words at that."[10] She then told readers that Peter Maurin had sought to make his words and his message dynamic by putting the corporal and spiritual works of mercy into practice on a daily basis, a practice that demanded personal sacrifice.

I. F. Stone, the muckraking Washington journalist, remarked after Dorothy's death that "of all the journalists of our generation, she wrote the best." In part that was because her articles were written from the trenches, from the slums where, in Pauline terms that she applied to herself, "the off-scouring of all" dwelt. As a result of her daily experience of living with the poor, Dorothy never trusted bureaucrats, who necessarily pigeonhole people, even as they are trying to assist them. She admired academics, but not those who, in the process of analyzing the poor, objectified them. Instead, her own writing about people is always lively, straightforward, and can be brutally honest. She once described an old carpenter at the Easton, Pennsylvania, farm.[11] He had come to them off the Bowery and had made not only the benches for the chapel, but also the altar. However, Maurice had a bitter tongue, Dorothy wrote, and he so despised the unskilled poor that "whenever anyone gave evidence of any skill, he would say sourly, 'And what jail did you learn that in?' "

Maurice's shop and his room were adjacent to the farm's entrance. But unlike the porter in St. Benedict's Rule, Maurice made few guests feel welcome. "I used to feel sad," Dorothy wrote, "that instead of seeing Christ in each guest who came, he saw the bum, and so treated us, one and all." He was, she said, a good example of *The Man Who Came to Dinner*. But he was also, she added, "a fitting member of our community, which is countrywide by now, and which Stanley Vishnewski has come to call 'the contemptibles.' " Once again, the saving grace of humor—and the ability to accept others where they are. The only way to change some people, Dorothy explained, was by one's own halting (and usually ineffective) example.

Kassie Temple, a brilliant *Catholic Worker* editor who died before her time in 2002, viewed the movement as a synthesis of the most traditional Catholic thought that had led to the most radical critique of modern society.[12] That critique applied not only to materialist and imperialist social systems, but to the church as well, which habitually wants to settle for the tepid gruel of worldly influence and success, and is in need of constant reform.

The very term "Catholic Worker" was a stumbling block for many. On first hearing it, some mistakenly associated it with the Communists' *Daily Worker*. For others, it was *too* Catholic. They saw it not as a radical critique of capitalism but as its ally in tattered clothing, intending to mislead the proletariat and maintain the church's privileged position. Still others felt it was not Catholic *enough*, boring from within at the heart and soul of Catholicism. This latter group of critics gradually faded away as the church caught up with papal social teaching and as the sincerity and orthodoxy of Dorothy and the Catholic Worker proved unassailable. But the criticisms of both capitalists and Communists endure, stung as they each are by the radical analysis of the Catholic Worker project.

It is an analysis based on the scriptural understanding that we are to earn our living by the sweat of our brows, not someone else's; and that whatever surplus we have should be shared with those in need. As Dorothy observed in 1969, "so much genius and hard labor are put forth in the interests of profit for the idle few, for the haves of our society, who have the money to invest, who know how to play around with money, make it increase, under our system. In the middle ages," she said, zeroing in on today's money-lending system, "lending at interest was considered a sin."[13]

When the Catholic Worker itself received a windfall check in 1960 of $3,579.39 from the City of New York for interest on a CW property the city had seized to build a subway,

Dorothy refused to accept it, and wrote to the city her reasons. The two great evils of our time, she said, quoting Eric Gill, were interest taking and war making. Nor would she apply for federal tax-exempt status or accept foundation grants. To do good works, particularly the works of mercy, she said, is a gospel imperative, one that has to be assumed freely. One did not feed the hungry or shelter the homeless to gain government approval or to claim a tax write-off. As for those potential foundation grants, they were to be refused because they were amassed at the expense of exploited workers or the environment. In contrast, the Catholic Worker relied entirely on small, freewill offerings, contributed by readers of the paper (who were reminded they could not take a tax exemption for their good deeds).

As for what to do if one felt he or she must invest money—and here Dorothy knew and respected the responsibility families have, particularly when it comes to the need to care for one's own—she advised searching out those investments that would provide for the needs of others, rather than investing for profit. Investing in housing for the poor, for example, was one good way "to make use of what God has put into [people's] hands." But the "very principle of using money to make money is wrong," she said.

What was put into Dorothy's hands usually came in small amounts and was directed to immediate needs, to paying down debts, and to assisting other CW houses. Gathering the money was something that fell almost entirely on Dorothy's shoulders, through her writing in the paper, her travels, and her speaking engagements. (There was never a set fee for her talks and frequently, no fee was offered. Sometimes she would talk at multiple Catholic schools on a given day but return home penniless.) The movement survived primarily through twice-a-year appeals, written by Dorothy and published in the paper and, if there was enough money, mailed to subscribers on newsprint. Getting up nerve to write them was one of Dorothy's most enduring challenges. "Here I am, groaning within at having to ask for money," she wrote in 1960. Still, the historian William D. Miller remarked, she could "put the bite on you" if she needed something—in his case, the family's extra car, a Datsun. The Broadway and film actress Carmen Mathews came to the rescue of the CW on several occasions, lending money in 1968 for the new First Street House. For a decade, Mathews would preside at the house's annual Christmas party, giving dramatic readings of old favorites like Dylan Thomas's *A Child's Christmas in Wales.*

Dorothy's appeal letters were sui generis, unique for their sincerity and straightforward, affectionate gratitude. They would begin "Dear Beloved Ones," or "Dear Fellow Workers in Christ," or simply, "Beloved (a warm word and I like to use it)." The appeals were both personal and personalist: they told stories of her and of those in need, but did so with complete respect for the latter. They seem to spring from— and be predicated on—her prayer and trust in God. Nonetheless, they realistically relied on the kindness of her readers. Dorothy was characteristically spontaneous in these letters. "We stopped [in a field near a cross] to say a prayer," she wrote in October 1951, "and I suddenly thought to pray for the $500 we needed to make a payment on the mortgage the following week. That very evening a friend came to us and told us he had the money for our use. God answers prayers. This we know." And then she resumed the appeal, "He answers them through you, our readers, and through the saints who watch over our work."

The appeals, usually published beneath a logo of loaves and fishes, would typically take up pressing issues and address questions readers might be asking. In 1966 she wrote that thanks to Peter Maurin, "we have been called to a life of voluntary poverty." But, she continued, "We know that there can be a natural attraction to poverty and the irresponsibility which goes with it. Artists, writers, musicians, and scientists have embraced poverty rather than the rewards of the world to follow their own vocation." Changing gears slightly, she wrote, "Surely it is a strange vocation to love the destitute and dissolute, those men sleeping in doorways, foul with the filth of the gutter, dying of drunkenness and malnutrition and fever and cold." This was followed, matter-of-factly, by "We have known many such deaths and have witnessed the depths of misery around us."

To identify with the poor—Dorothy had been doing it for more than thirty years by that time—was not only a "curious vocation" but "a blessing." In 1968 she wrote, "The wolf is at the door daily, but we are so used to him that we'd miss him if he were not there." She told of the young people who came to the Worker to volunteer, but who themselves needed help. Scarred by the Vietnam War and violence in the streets, "they find their healing by throwing in their lot with ours." She concluded with: "We can only pray daily to God, 'Give me your love, so that I will have love to give, unjudging and unquestioning love.'" She ended yet another letter simply, "May we all be joyful in the Lord, God."

Dorothy liked to quote St. Hilary: "The less you have of Caesar's, the less you have to render Caesar."[14] Not only was voluntary poverty to be sought in imitation of Christ, but living poorly meant one would have less to do with "the all-encroaching state." She saw her times as those of the totalitarian state: "We've had Stalin's dictatorship, Hitler's dictatorship, Mussolini's dictatorship," she remarked in a 1972 interview. "We don't realize that we're going into the same kind of thing." Speaking against the Smith and Mc-Carran Acts twenty years before, she had rightly said citizens will not be made loyal by mere loyalty oaths. As she told her audience: "We will not defend democracy by repressive laws."

Her impulse to stand against the state, and her willingness to suffer the consequences, were consistent themes throughout Dorothy's life. Her speech to the Liberal-Socialist Alliance, the day after Pearl Harbor, is a clarion example. "War must cease," she said. "The world can bear the burden no longer. Yes, we must take a stand."

Half a year later while traveling on the West Coast, Dorothy was appalled at finding the camps the government had set up for Japanese Americans. As she told *Catholic Worker* readers in June 1942: "I saw a bit of Germany on the West Coast. I saw some of the concentration camps where the Japanese men, women, and children are being held before they are being resettled." The strange part of this "wholesale imprisonment of an innocent people," she wrote, "is that many of them are native born citizens of this country. But that means nothing in wartime." She reported that the spirit of the Japanese was "one of helpless misery. They are the first victims of war in this country, and if we did not cry out against the injustice done them, if we did not protest it, we would be failing in two of the works of mercy—which are to visit the prisoner and ransom the captive."

In the same issue of the paper, Dorothy reported what she had discovered at Our Lady of Lourdes Church in West Seattle. The church was situated on a hill, overlooking a Boeing aircraft factory. Within a hundred feet of her, she said, was a huge barrage balloon, and tents had been set up nearby for soldiers. On the other side of the church, in what she called "a lovely monastery garden," she observed a machine gun nest and an anti-aircraft nest, camouflaged and surrounded by sandbags. "I do not doubt but that if the army wanted the bell tower of any church in America, they would be moving right in," she reported.

In the following issue of the paper, July–August 1942, Dorothy told of having received a letter from the Office of Censorship in Washington, DC. They had objected to her story on the Japanese, but also to "our calling attention (naming locations) of anti-aircraft nests on the West Coast." The exchange of letters was cordial, she said. "We apologized for our indiscretion . . . and they thanked us." But, she added, "We are forced to repeat our protest at the presence of anti-aircraft batteries or some kind of camps along our waterfronts on the property of Catholic institutions." She had only recently discovered such installations at a Catholic institution on the East Coast. The War Department had confiscated six acres of church property, she said, "at a rental of a dollar for the duration of the war."

This was a forthright questioning of US government policy during the war, an argument for the separation of church and state, a testimony to the primacy of conscience and the freedom of the press. Dorothy's concern for the Japanese Americans detained during the war was prophetic. The need for some recompense for them was only belatedly recognized—decades later by the larger society and the government. The Catholic Worker was one of the few outspoken voices for Catholic conscientious objectors during World War II. It sponsored a poorly run, desperately underfinanced camp in Warner, New Hampshire, for Catholics who had been granted CO status.

With the Armageddon-like ending of the war, Dorothy wrote a searing appraisal of the new atomic age in the *Catholic Worker:*

Mr. Truman was jubilant. President Truman. True man; what a strange name, come to think of it. We refer to Jesus Christ as true God and true Man. Truman is a man of his time in that he was jubilant . . . *Jubilate Deo*. We have killed 318,000 Japanese.

That is, we hope we have killed them. . . . The effect is hoped for, not known. It is to be hoped they are vaporized, our Japanese brothers, scattered—men, women, and babies—to the four winds over the seven seas. Perhaps we will breathe their dust into our nostrils, feel them in the fog of New York in our faces, feel them in the rain. . . .

Today's paper with its columns of description of the new era, the atomic era, which this colossal slaughter of innocents has ushered in, is filled with stories covering every conceivable phase of the new discovery. Pictures of the towns and industrial plants where the parts are made are spread across the pages. In the forefront of the town of Oak Ridge, Tennessee, is a chapel, a large comfortable looking chapel benignly settled beside the plant. And the scientists making the first tests in the desert prayed, one newspaper account said.

Yes, God is still in the picture. God is not mocked. . . . We are held in God's hands, all of us, and President Truman too, and these scientists who have created death. . . . He, God, holds our life and our happiness, our sanity, and our health; our lives are in His hands.

He is our Creator. Creator. . . .

Everyone says, "I wonder what the pope thinks of it?" How everyone turns to the Vatican for judgment, even though they do not seem to listen to the voices there! But Our Lord Himself has already pronounced judgment of the atomic bomb. When James and John (John the beloved) wished to call down fire from heaven on their enemies, Jesus said:

"You know not what spirit you are. The Son of Man came not to destroy souls but to save."[15]

Dorothy herself refused to pay federal income taxes because so much went for wars—past, current, and future. As it was, she had so little personal income it was undoubtedly a moot question. Born well before the advent of Social Security, she neither applied for it nor received it. Still, she publicly declared her unwillingness to pay the income tax and encouraged others to follow suit. Some did and paid the price—in jail or through garnished wages. When she learned of this, she would congratulate them: "The impulse to stand out against the state and go to jail . . . is an instinct for penance—to take some of the suffering of the world, to share in it," she wrote in 1969.[16] (The Catholic Worker pays local taxes on the principles of subsidiarity and solidarity, and a willingness to pay for services rendered in one's neighborhood.)

In 1952 Dorothy had told her Carnegie Hall audience that the Treasury had so far refrained from coming after her, but in 1971 that changed. The Vietnam War was raging and the Catholic Worker was conspicuously active in the antiwar movement. "The federal income tax people are on our heels," she wrote to her biographer William D. Miller. "They class us as a political group, not a charitable one, which is paying us a great compliment—we are indeed trying to do more fundamental things for justice and peace than feed a soup line."[17] ("*Not* to have the government pay attention to you," she told the editors of *Sojourners* in 1976, "is almost a sign you're not doing anything.")[18]

Early in 1972 the Internal Revenue Service assessed the Catholic Worker three hundred thousand dollars for nonpayment of income taxes over the previous six years. Dorothy countered that the CW did not pay income taxes because it did not pay salaries (the ongoing significance of Peter Maurin's "work, not wages"). That spring, Dorothy took the pulse of the community on how best to respond to the IRS threat. But she seemed to have already concluded what to do if the government confiscated the Catholic Worker's holdings and bank account. Should that happen, she and the other members of the community would simply get odd jobs and continue the work out of their tenement apartments. If the *CW* paper were to be suppressed, she said the editors would turn to leafleting and hand distribution. They would not be deterred.

In 1959 the movement had been thrown out of its home at the time, 223 Chrystie Street. For the next ten years it rented dilapidated storefronts and tenement apartments. Yet the work continued. Dorothy observed, "This is the way we began back in 1933. . . . and we have gone back to our beginnings, which is a healthy thing. Certainly there is not much chance of the Catholic Worker movement becoming static."[19]

In that spirit Dorothy faced possible confiscation and eviction during the Nixon era. She understood that her refusal to cooperate with the government opened her to criticisms from a variety of perspectives, including from house residents as well as readers. "I am sure that many will think me a fool," she wrote in May 1972, "for jeopardizing the work on behalf of this principle."[20] That June, in a face-to-face meeting with William Hunter (an assistant US attorney general who had come up from Washington), she made her case. "The point of the matter is this: we are paying for war if we pay the tax. It is so important for us to hold our stance, even if," she added, "the government lowers the boom."[21] In conclusion she told Mr. Hunter: "We have an absolute faith that we will keep going even if we lose everything. Our principle is what we are living for."

"I think Mr. Hunter shared with us," Dorothy wrote, "the conviction that you could not kill an idea, and that we would continue to express ourselves and live the Catholic Worker positions as best we could, no matter what steps were taken against us by the government. To *resist* and to *survive*," she concluded.[22]

It seemed the government came to understand Dorothy's resolve, and that it took note of the opprobrium being heaped on it by the national press for its threat to shut down the Catholic Worker. What was remarkable to me at the time was Dorothy's calmness in the midst of this storm and her directness with the government's representative. As John Henry Newman had observed in a sermon a century before, "It is a difficult and rare virtue to mean what we say, to love without dissimulation, to think no evil, to bear no grudge, to be free of selfishness, to be innocent and straightforward." In the meeting with Mr. Hunter, Dorothy acquitted herself on all these grounds. The guileless person, Newman went on, "has a simple boldness" and is able to overcome dangers others shrink from "because they have no danger for him, and thus he gains even worldly advantages, by his straight-forwardness."[23] On July 11, 1972, the IRS sent the Catholic Worker a terse notice stating that the case had been closed.

CHAPTER FIVE

Catholicity and Lady Poverty

In early 1960, more than two years before the opening session of the Second Vatican Council, Dorothy wrote in her column about an article she had been reading in *America*. It was by the Jesuit theologian Gustave Weigel, who argued there were three areas the church in the United States needed to address: (1) austerity, preached and lived; (2) a deeper awareness of the reality of God; and (3) a truer, more effective love of all people, "including those who are our enemies."[1] For Dorothy, the list might not have stopped there—and no doubt, Weigel would have agreed. But the three areas he pointed to were ones the Catholic Worker had been stressing from the beginning: poverty, the primacy of the spiritual, and nonviolence/love of enemy.

Aware of both its achievements and failures, Dorothy clearly had a deep love for the church. She understood Péguy's dictum that the bond between saints and sinners is basic: that the sinner "lies at the heart of Christianity."[2] Dorothy's broad understanding of the church, its history, and its saints allowed her to navigate within the church in a way that its structures never restricted or compromised her integrity and freedom.

The theologian Rosemary Haughton, who met Dorothy in the 1970s, caught this uncommon breadth in *The Catholic Thing* (1979). There Haughton lays out the range, rich tradition, and freedom of Catholicism as exemplified in such teachers and models as Augustine, Heloise, Erasmus, Newman, Baron Friedrich von Hügel, and Dorothy Day. According to Haughton, Dorothy contributed a new clarity and direction for the church. "Only such an enterprise" as Catholicism, Haughton wrote, "could have satisfied Dorothy Day, or been able to include her without destroying or suppressing her."[3]

During remarks at Spode House in England in the fall of 1963, Dorothy said that wherever she spoke, the audience invariably asked her: "What is the attitude of the church to the Catholic Worker?" "Well, I say, we are an example of the tremendous liberty that there is in the church." Further, "the layman should go ahead and quit being dependent and priest-ridden." The fact of the matter, she advised, was that "you don't need permission to form your conscience." She added that E. I. Watkin, the British theologian, wrote "you have to follow your conscience even if it takes you out of the church."[4] As Dorothy put it later in her talk, "We must have the courage to form our conscience and follow it, regardless of the point of view of cardinal or bishop." Recalling that a bishop had told Peter Maurin, "You lead the way and we'll follow," she said that the Catholic Worker had taken the bishop at his word.

The idea was to try to build new institutions, to find new ways of dealing with social problems, and not to be afraid of making mistakes. Dorothy continued, "We learn by them, we learn the hard way," but "we don't involve the church in these mistakes." When it came to the issues of peace, justice, and the economy, she said, "we are exploring all

Catholic points of view with regard to these things," and other points of view as well, "whether it be communists, anarchists, socialists, or whoever." For "the truth is the truth and proceeds from the Holy Spirit, and so we follow it wherever we find it." Dorothy noted in her talk that Cardinal Paul-Émile Léger of Montreal had once asked her what was the Catholic Worker's "juridical position" in the church ("I think that was the expression he used," she said). "And I said we have none at all of course."

"This business of 'asking Father' what to do about something," Dorothy wrote in a 1964 article, "has never occurred to us."[5] Yet she also described how, when the *Catholic Worker* was first getting started, she had approached three priest advisors (all of them editors) and questioned them whether she should seek ecclesiastical permission. She said all three told her "to launch out, but not to ask permission. It would not be given, it was implied." This advice seems to have proven providential, for it gave the Catholic Worker Movement a freedom that has served it and the church well for the better part of a century.

In 1951 Msgr. Edward Gaffney of the Archdiocese of New York wrote to Dorothy strongly suggesting that she and the movement stop using the title "Catholic Worker." In a nuanced and wily response—which included equal parts deference and resolve—Dorothy reminded the monsignor that the movement was just as entitled to using the term "Catholic" as the Catholic War Veterans were, and that the CW had been doing so for eighteen years without previous objection. To remove "Catholic" from the paper and the movement now would be "to give scandal around the world," Dorothy wrote, and "put into the hands of our enemies, the enemies of the Church, a formidable weapon."[6] The argument apparently chastened the archdiocese. There was never another attempt to strip the Catholic Worker of its name.

Dorothy also told her Spode House audience (1963) that some bishops had not welcomed her or the *Catholic Worker*, although they had allowed individuals in their jurisdiction to read the paper. Then she told the story of the current bishop of San Diego, California, who had recently refused to allow a group of theologians, priests, monsignori, and the journalist John Cogley to speak in his diocese. Every time she herself had been invited there, she said, the same bishop had canceled the meeting. "Some sisters would invite me and suddenly the meeting would be canceled. Some priests would invite me to their parish; the meeting would be canceled." But then, she recalled, "a lay group would have to get together and find a meeting place." They would simply go to the house of a lay person and have the gathering there, and the laity and the clergy would all show up.

When Dorothy had returned to New York from San Diego, the same bishop had sent her a check for two hundred or two hundred and fifty dollars—she wasn't quite sure which—and everyone around the office asked her, "What is this—conscience money?" But Dorothy didn't see it that way. "I would say it was an indication that he thoroughly approved our going ahead, and that he wished other people would go ahead without asking permission," she said. "I would say that the clergy should be very happy and probably are very happy that we are instigating a movement among the laity of going ahead on our own." Indeed, it was a new model of doing things in the church, but one based on the authority of the gospels and the freedom of the Holy Spirit. As the apostle Paul told the Ephesians (2:19), "You are no longer strangers and aliens, but you are citizens with the saints." The Catholic Worker understood this and acted on it. In his posthumously published book *The One-Man Revolution in America* (1970), Ammon Hennacy wrote that one of the many remarkable things about Dorothy was that she had chosen to remain in the Catholic Church, battling from *inside* what he called "an autocratic and corrupt organization, and by her life encourage others to fight their battles in a peaceful way. She chose only pure weapons," he added, and because of that, "she stands as one of the most basic of radicals."[7]

Dorothy reminded Catholics that, among other things, the Italian unificationists Giuseppe Garibaldi and Giuseppe Mazzini—who confiscated the Papal States—were "instruments of God" by "relieving the church of the burden of property." She advised religious congregations to break up their large land holdings. In 1968 she wrote Gordon Zahn, the sociologist and World War II Catholic conscientious objector (he later discovered and publicized the heroic story of now Blessed Franz Jägerstätter, the Austrian Catholic who refused to serve in Hitler's army and was executed): "As a convert, I never expected much of the bishops. In all history popes and bishops and father abbots seem to have been blind and power loving and greedy. I never expected leadership from them. It is the saints who keep appearing throughout history who keep things going. What I do expect is the bread of life and down through the ages there is that continuity. . . . The Gospel is hard. Loving your enemies, and the worst are of your own household, is hard."[8]

Dorothy learned this early on when it came to addressing the issue of Catholic anti-Semitism. In 1933 she had submitted an article to *America* decrying anti-Semitism among the American Catholic laity. The editor—a friend—Wilfrid Parsons, SJ, had rejected the article. (*America* belatedly published it in 2009.) Hitler had come to power that year, and the catastrophic persecution of the Jews had already begun in Germany. As Dorothy wrote in her submission to Fr. Parsons, the editors of the *Catholic Worker* had previously decided not to venture into writing about world affairs, but when they discovered Catholics getting up on New York streets to "arouse race hatred in their Catholic listeners," she noted, "then it is time for us to take a stand."

"It is the pogrom spirit being revived," Dorothy said, and compared anti-Semitism to the persecution of the Negro in the United States "because of his race." As was typical of her style and method, she then related having recently seen anti-Semitism combated on the streets of New York. "The other day we had a German Protestant livery stableman giving us the use of a horse and wagon to move a Jewish family [which had been evicted], and five Catholic unemployed men assisting their brother the Jew in getting transference. It is a situation which typifies the point I wish to make," she wrote, "that we are all creatures of God and members or potential members of the Mystical Body. This is something which those Catholics who bait the Jews lose sight of."

Dorothy felt that the Sermon on the Mount and the "counsels of perfection" were meant for all Christians. In her early book *House of Hospitality*, she observed "it is sad that it is always the minimum that is expected of lay people." But, she noted, the times called for a "new technique," one in which the laity must "make use of the spiritual weapons at our disposal, and by hard work, sacrifice, self-discipline, patience, and prayer (and we won't have any of the former without the latter), work from day to day in the tasks that present themselves." That could mean combating anti-Semitism or racism on the streets, finding housing for the evicted, clothing the naked, or simply feeding the hungry.

"We have a program of action and a philosophy of life," she said, and "the thing is to use them." At which point she turned her critical eye on the Catholic Worker itself: "We get too much praise from some for performing work which is our plain duty," she said. "Indeed, we deserve censure for not having done more."[9]

Georges Bernanos, the French author, noted that "the saints were obedient, not docile." Kate Hennessy, Dorothy's youngest granddaughter, wrote on the twenty-fifth anniversary of Dorothy's death that she was sure her grandmother "was an obedient daughter of the church," but that her "definitions of obedience and of the church were wide and vibrant, and in many ways not the world of the church hierarchy."[10] Dorothy once counseled a Jesuit scholastic that when you take a vow of obedience, you have to go ahead and obey, even when it's difficult, knowing that "God can straighten things out." We have to have "an increase of faith," she said, that "God would raise up somebody who will do it better. And that is why I think obedience is a supreme act of faith." Then, in her paradoxical, almost dialectical manner, she continued, "I think you can't go against your conscience." In the end, she said, conscience might dictate leaving religious life or the priesthood.[11] And when it came to the laity, she would quote Vatican II's *De Ecclesia*, "On the Church" (37): "They are obliged to speak up to express their opinion when something concerns the good of the church."

When Jeff Dietrich of the *Catholic Agitator* asked Dorothy in 1971 how she dealt with bishops, she simply replied, "I think you approach a bishop as a human being and a member of the human family. St. Peter betrayed Christ three times," she observed. "Christ just chose someone who was weak and faulty."[12] This acceptance of human frailty, and an acknowledgment of her own vicissitudes, made Dorothy's readers feel a ready bond with her. They could identify with her failures and worries, some of which seemed even amusing.

Invited to attend a special congress of the lay apostolate in Rome in 1967, Dorothy and an American astronaut were chosen to represent the United States and to receive Communion from the pope. As she described the experience in her column, she was seated with fellow communicants off to the side of the main altar, where they were sequestered until finally directed to approach the pope. What she noticed was not the glory of Michelangelo's dome or the brilliance of Bernini's baldachino, but the transparent tape on the floor: "A thoughtful piece of housekeeping to keep the cardinals from stumbling," she wrote. And added, "I may say that I was very preoccupied with whether I was going to stumble." Then she put the honor of receiving Communion from the pope in context. "Of course, I was happy at the Mass, feeling as I did that I was representing the men from our soup line, the pickets from Delano and all Cesar Chavez's fellow workers in California and Texas, and the little babies and small children of the agricultural workers who are present at our own farm in Tivoli in the day-care center."[13] The church was a worldwide communion, experienced in the sharing and partaking of the bread of life.

Dorothy was fond of repeating that one must live in a state of perpetual dissatisfaction with the church. After a searing 1967 column criticizing Cardinal Spellman and other churchmen for blessing the ongoing war in Vietnam, she put the ecclesial issue in a more immediate, personal perspective: "As to the church, where else shall we go, except to the bride of Christ, one flesh with Christ? Though she is a harlot at times, she is our Mother."[14] Dorothy looked at the church— and Christianity—with a long-term perspective: "A thousand years are as one day in the sight of the Lord," she wrote in

1960 (quoting 2 Peter 3:8), and "Christianity is only two days old."[15] This gave her not only hope, but determination.

As for those who should be chosen to be bishops, Dorothy felt that ordinary priests who had spoken publicly for the poor and paid the price deserved that call. In 1961 while traveling to Louisiana, she wrote of Fr. Jerome Drolet, whose picture had appeared in the *New York Times* the previous year, standing up to crowds protesting integrated schools in New Orleans. She had known Drolet since 1937 when he had worked briefly at the Catholic Worker in support of striking seamen. Later, as a priest in Louisiana, he had worked with sugar cane workers, and he had run a house of hospitality in Houma. There he had also opened an integrated ballpark and playground for children. Yet time and again, whenever Fr. Drolet made his voice heard, he had been transferred. "I often think what good bishops these young priests would make," Dorothy said. She suggested that "being transferred all over the diocese, they get to know it as few others can."[16]

Dorothy wanted bishops to be involved in all the works of mercy, physical and spiritual, and in the works of justice. While jailed for the farm workers' cause near Fresno, California, in 1973, she told Gerard Sherry of the *National Catholic Reporter* that she hoped some bishops "would come to the valley and to the other areas of the country where the farm workers are struggling for their rights," putting themselves "squarely on the side of the poor and oppressed."[17]

But Dorothy's argument was not simply with clerics or specifically with the hierarchy. As she noted in a diary entry in early 1969: "Necessary for people to change. Quit worrying about popes, cardinals, bishops, structures, institutions." When Msgr. Stephen J. Kelleher of the Archdiocese of New York wrote her in March 1966 asking for her thoughts on renewing canon law in light of the documents of Vatican II, she commended him for consulting the laity, as Cardinal Newman had suggested. She then frankly admitted, "I know nothing of canon law," but added in light of recent advancements in Catholic Scripture studies that "it certainly seems to me that canon law should be considered in light of Scripture, in the light of the new dispensation of love, rather than law." This should apply particularly in the realms of "education, marriage, and the status of women, church and state, war and peace," where, "it seems to me, the laity have much to say." At the bottom of her copy of the letter, however, in her own hand, are the words, "unanswered. Heard no more."

As for answers, at least when it came to a number of church teachings and to the counsels of perfection, Dorothy argued, "There are always answers, although they are not calculated to soothe."[18] She noted in 1962 (well before Paul VI's *Humanae Vitae*), "In the life of the family, heroic virtue is expected, in accepting from the hand of God each child sent or accepting continence or celibacy within marriage." Furthermore, "the teaching of the church in response to marriage and indissolubility demands over and again heroic sanctity."[19] "We fall far short of everything we profess," she wrote two years later, "but we certainly don't want to water down the doctrine of Christ to fit ourselves. . . . We have to do our share. For the rest, 'His grace is sufficient for us.' "[20]

When Scott Nearing, the radical economist and back-to-the-land pioneer, and his granddaughter visited Dorothy in February 1964, she wondered aloud in her diary: "Why are non-Catholics and nonreligious people so good—so much better than RCs?" Despite all the failures of individual Catholics and of the institution, however, Dorothy maintained that the church bore within itself "the seeds of its own regeneration."[21] That regeneration would happen only when the seed had fallen into the ground and died. To continue to live each day in faithfulness and constancy—that is what was/is essential. Concomitantly, for Dorothy the loss of faith would constitute the greatest tragedy in a person's life.

In her letter to Msgr. Kelleher in 1966, Dorothy concluded by saying that the defining problem the church faces is poverty. She told the monsignor that over the years poverty was the issue that "the Catholic Worker has had the most to say, and is least understood." The problem is "more fundamental," she added, "than the problem of war."

"What is the meaning of poverty within the church?" Cardinal Giacomo Lercaro of Bologna had asked during Vatican II (a speech reprinted in the September 1963 *Catholic Worker*). "It was chosen by the incarnate Son of God," the cardinal said, a "choice he constantly maintained throughout his life, from the stable in Bethlehem to the cross. What is more, he preached poverty and held it forth as an inescapable demand for those who wished to be his disciples." All the great reforms in the church, the cardinal explained, had taken place when the church had rediscovered and rededicated itself to the poverty of Jesus.

These were the very issues Dorothy had tried to draw to Msgr. Kelleher's attention. She and Peter Maurin had addressed them from the start; poverty was a constant and consistent subject of her writing and speeches. "While there are slums, we must live in them and share the condition of the poor," she wrote in the April 1958 issue of the paper. "Poverty is so esteemed by God it is something to be sought after, worked for, the pearl of great price" (July–August, 1953). Why? "Let us love to live with the poor because they are especially loved by Christ," and "We cannot even see our brothers in need without first stripping ourselves." In a

1950 diary entry, Dorothy calls poverty "our greatest message: to be poor with the poor." Again in 1959, she writes, "the foundations are always in poverty, manual labor, and in seeming failure. It is the pattern of the cross, and in the cross is joy of spirit."

The poverty that the Catholic Worker espouses is not destitution, although it has sometimes seemed very near to it. (When Maisie Ward visited the CW house on Mott Street soon after arriving in the United States, she called it "a slum within a slum.") "In what does our poverty consist?" Dorothy asked herself in 1961. "In toilets out of commission in town, dish washers who wipe their noses on the dishtowels, people who are mental cases."[22] While this is obviously a very incomplete description of poverty lived among the poor, it does hint at what such a calling might entail.

In one of her appeal letters (October 1957), Dorothy described a man lying outside St. Joseph House one evening, beneath a beautiful stone statue of St. Joseph cradling the child Jesus (it had been carved by the Minnesota sculptor Joseph O'Connell). She said she had often seen passersby reverence the statue: men would tip their hats, "and sometimes old Italian women curtsey and kiss their fingers . . . and show other signs of appreciation of his friendship to our house of hospitality." And then Dorothy described the man lying on the street, "close up against our house, his knees up to his chest, his head on his arm. He was asleep. An Italian woman who could not speak English kept pointing to the man saying in turn, 'Jesus Christ . . . my son, my heart is broken.'"

"He wasn't really her son," Dorothy wrote, "but she knew what she was talking about. He *was* Jesus Christ, shocking as it may seem, drunk as he was. That was part of the agony in the garden, when He took our sins and all the sins that would be committed upon Himself. People are always see-ing this truth for the first time."

"Our poverty is *not* a stark and dreary poverty," Dorothy wrote in 1939, "because we have the security which living together brings." Nonetheless, it could include overcrowd-ing, a lack of privacy, no hot water, "bedbugs and cock-roaches and rats and the constant war against these."[23] It also meant a lack of paint, soap, and cleaning powders. Still, Catholic Worker poverty was not without its joys. As her granddaughter Kate recalled, Dorothy had a knack for turn-ing "the life of poverty into something dynamic, full of richly simple moments for those who have nothing."[24] As Dorothy put it herself, "It is always a feast where love is, and where love is, God is."[25]

Voluntary poverty needs to be preached and esteemed for other reasons as well: so employees won't be afraid of losing their jobs if they speak out on issues and so pastors and congregations won't be afraid of losing the support of rich benefactors. "A readiness for poverty, a disposition to accept it, is enough to begin with," Dorothy wrote in 1964.[26] And five years later she encouraged readers to embark on this path themselves, reminding them that an act of love, "a voluntary taking on oneself of some of the pain of the world, increases the courage and love and hope of all."[27]

When asked one Lent how she could see Christ in other people, Dorothy responded, "It is an act of faith, constantly repeated. It is an act of love, resulting from an act of faith. It is an act of hope, that we can awaken these same acts in their hearts, too."[28] And then she briefly analyzed the three theological virtues in practice:

> How do we know we believe? How do we know we indeed
> have faith? Because we have seen his hands and his feet in

the poor around us. He has shown himself to us in them. We start by loving them for him, and soon we love them for themselves, each one a unique person, most special!

It is most surely an exercise of faith for us to see Christ in each other. But it is through such exercises that we grow, and the joy of our vocation assures us we are on the right path.

Dorothy told young people who came to live at the Catholic Worker that "you will know your vocation by the joy that it brings you." It was clear that her vocation to the Catholic Worker—and to a life of poverty—had brought her such freedom and joy. Practically, this meant she had to keep trying to divest herself of things. "Upon reading Trollope's *The Warden* this month," she noted in March 1969, "I realize how acquisitive each of us are [*sic*], not only of books, radios for concerts, but of time and loving kindness." While aware of her own acquisitive nature, she was perennially self-effacing about what she and the CW had achieved: "We were saying last night [during the 1937 seamen's strike] that if we could have foreseen the hordes that were to come to us the past two months, we would never have had the courage to begin. But we can only work day to day."

As to the question of what were the causes of the tremendous gap between the rich and the poor, Dorothy answered in February 1965: "One can't answer this question without taking into consideration the entire history of the United States, man's nature, his fall and redemption. To put it simply, the root cause of the gap is man's greed, avarice, acquisitiveness, his fear of insecurity, and lack of attention to the teachings of Jesus and the saints throughout the ages."

Dorothy seemed tireless in quoting those saints. Here is St. Ambrose: "You are not making a gift of your possessions to the poor person. You are handing over to him what is his.

For what has been given in common for the use of all, you have arrogated to yourself. The world is given to all, and not only to the rich."[29] And St. Gregory the Great: "When we attend to the needs of those in want, we give them what is theirs, not ours. More than performing works of mercy, we are paying a debt in justice."[30] In 1976 Dorothy told the editors of *Sojourners* that she had been asked to talk to the bishops of the United States on two occasions in recent years, and that she had advised them, "Don't invest money, except in the poor—there you might expect a return."

Jacques Maritain, whose book *True Humanism* was studied assiduously by the early Catholic Workers, had written that "to apply the social doctrine of the [papal] encyclicals effectively, there is one essential—to live with the masses."[31] On the occasion of Dorothy's seventy-fifth birthday, John Cogley wrote in the *New York Times* that she "had proven her devotion to the poor by being poor herself." He then broadened the picture: "She has demonstrated her dedication to peace, time and again, by going to jail. She has strengthened the cause of women, not by haranguing men but by actually leading them, in the most rigid of male monopolies, the Roman Catholic Church. . . . [She] not only changed her friends and admirers, she changed American Catholicism itself. And she did it by 'working within the system.' "[32] As Dorothy had admonished herself and her coworkers in 1961, putting the whole question of poverty and war in perspective, "We are not going to win the masses to Christ until we live it."[33]

CHAPTER SIX

Peace and the Primacy of the Spiritual

To assume a life of Catholic Worker poverty meant to gradually put concerns about daily sustenance and provision in perspective. But these quotidian concerns pale before the gut fear and anxiety generated by exposure to violence and the threat of it—whether from random acts or from war and civil unrest. In 1975 Dorothy wrote that the young people who came to volunteer at the CW learned not only how to love with compassion, "but to overcome fear, that dangerous emotion that precipitates violence."[1] They may go on feeling fear, she noted, but their experience of non-violence at the Catholic Worker and their personal growth in faith gave them the means to overcome their fear.

Overcoming fear, "the fear of one's enemies," Dorothy emphasized, was an essential challenge and a lifelong process. In 1957 when she was shot at while standing vigil at Koinonia in Georgia, she said it was only prayer that steadied her knees and helped her overcome her shaking. She drew attention to the Scriptures: "Do not fear for I am with you" (Isa 43:5); "Do not be afraid, little flock" (Luke 12:32);

and "Perfect love casts out fear" (1 John 4:18). In 1963 she was in Danville, Virginia, and heard Martin Luther King Jr. speak. He told a large audience that he had seen police brutality before, but seldom on such a scale as had happened in Danville the previous week. Black men, women, and children—demonstrating for their civil and human rights—had been brutally beaten by the police, dragged through the streets, stripped, and their limbs broken.

A week later Dorothy was asked to speak at a mass meeting at a Baptist church in Danville. She had just been in Rome and so talked about Pope John XXIII's recent encyclical *Pacem in Terris* and what it had to say about the rights of conscience, unjust laws, and the place of women in the world. She finished by praising the congregants' nonviolent resistance, their members' willingness to lay down their lives for their brothers and sisters, "colored and white." She admitted in her report in the July–August 1963 *Catholic Worker* that, prior to speaking, she had prayed to be delivered from her own fear, and that "I do not know whether I would have had the courage to speak, outsider that I was, had not the singing lightened my own heart, dissolved my own fear."

A cardinal rule was that pacifism and nonviolence should never be undertaken out of cowardice. "We must love our enemy," Dorothy said, "not because we fear war but because God loves him."[2] Years earlier, when Mike Wallace asked her whether "God loves murderers, a Hitler, a Stalin?" she could only respond: "God loves all men, and all men are brothers."[3] This credo is reflected in a handwritten leaflet Dorothy composed when refusing to take shelter during the civil-defense drills:

> We are all responsible for what our country is doing in stockpiling and preparing to use nuclear weapons. We are

guilty of what America did when our country bombed Hiroshima and Nagasaki. So we refuse to take part in this war game—this compulsory civil defense drill in which we are ordered to take cover. . . . There is no defense, there is no escape, there is no shelter in a nuclear war.

War is murder and suicide, Pope Pius XII said. It would follow that to participate in war or war games is to be a part of this sin of murder and suicide. So we are disobeying the law. By this act of civil disobedience and accepting its penalty, we are trying to do penance and atone for our sin.

What will happen if we disarm, if "Russia takes over"? Better to die loving our enemies, as Jesus Christ told us to, than to die carrying our fellowmen with us to the grave. Why not die laying down our lives for our fellows?[4]

"'Love your enemies' is the hardest saying of all," Dorothy told Irish-born war protester Michael Cullen in 1970.[5] He was preparing to serve a prison sentence for his part in an antiwar action in Milwaukee. "It is a terrible thought—'We love God as much as the one we love least,'" she said, and then added a prayer for herself: "Please, Father in heaven who made me, take away my heart of stone and give me a heart of flesh to love my enemy." It was such an awareness and witness that led people like John Cogley to reflect: "It has made it impossible for nonpacifists like me to accept violence unthinkingly."[6]

In 1973 Dorothy told the *National Catholic Reporter* that she had been mugged twice (once in New York and once in Chicago). As a result, "when I'm out at night I walk nearer the curb than the house." She then related how on one of these occasions, her assailants grabbed her around the neck as she was entering her apartment building. After robbing her they told her, "Get in and shut up." But Dorothy had the presence of mind to demand, "Give me my pocketbook with my keys in it. I can't get in." So they reluctantly handed back her purse and fled down the alley. "I opened my pocketbook inside under the light," she recalled. "I was shaking. There was a twenty-dollar bill they hadn't found!"[7]

Robert Bresson, the filmmaker who directed such classics as *Diary of a Country Priest* and *Au hazard Balthazar*, remarked "the supernatural is only the real brought up close."[8] In it we live and move and have our being, but aren't cognizant of it. Thus, the practice of the presence of God—making ourselves attentive to God in every aspect of our lives—was a key element of what Peter Maurin called "the primacy of the spiritual." "This work of ours toward a new heaven and a new earth," Dorothy wrote in 1940, "shows a correlation between the material and the spiritual, and, of course, recognizes the primacy of the spiritual."[9] Food for the body is not enough, she said. "There must be food for the soul."

Dorothy insisted that since "we live in a time of gigantic evil," it was hopeless to combat it "by any other means than that of sanctity."[10] That obviously meant making every effort to change the social order, but it also understood that transforming oneself came first. "To think of overcoming such evil by material means—by alleviations, by changes to the social order—all this is utterly hopeless," she said. She spelled this out repeatedly, encouraging young people at the Catholic Worker to go to Mass daily: "Scripture, on the one hand, and the Eucharist, the Word made flesh, on the other," she wrote in 1972, "have in them the strength which no power on earth can withstand."[11] The Mass, she had written in 1938, "is the most important work of the day. . . . If I can just remember to do that well—as well as I am able— everything else will take care of itself."[12] As ever, her practicality and self-awareness: "*as well as I am able*."

In her copy of Julian of Norwich's *Revelation of Divine Love*, Dorothy underlined Christ's address to Julian: "Because I love you, enjoy me! This will please me most of all." As Dorothy often said, it was joy at the birth of her child that brought her to God; on Christmas Day, 1961, she noted that that same sense of "joy is constantly renewed as I receive Our Lord at Mass."[13]

From its earliest days the Catholic Worker was involved in the liturgical movement—the renewal of Catholic prayer life and ritual that would be given an emphatic impetus at Vatican II. Dorothy was close to Virgil Michel, OSB, who saw the essential relationship between the liturgy and the church's social teaching; Msgr. Martin Hellriegel of St. Louis, who worked to incorporate the congregation's participation in the Mass; Fr. Robert Hovda, a World War II conscientious objector and convert who fused liturgy with Christ's teaching on peace and reconciliation; and Dom Godfrey Diekmann, OSB, the longtime editor of *Worship*.

In 1939, twelve years after having become a Catholic, Dorothy made the first of what would be numerous retreats inspired by a French-Canadian Jesuit, Onesimus Lacouture. "At last I have found what I was looking for when I left my communist friends and became a Catholic," she told her friend Sr. Peter Claver Fahy. It was a gospel-centered spirituality that encouraged retreatants to make the "counsels of perfection" an integral part of their moral and spiritual lives. Dorothy called the retreat "the bread of the strong" and "the great retreat," and said it gave those who made it "new meaning and vigor," a renewed sense of "hope and courage."

Dorothy described going to meet Fr. Lacouture years later in Sudbury, Ontario. The retreat had already been branded with a reputation for being overly rigorous—seven days of silence, five conferences a day, with an emphasis on Christ's passion and the taking up of one's own cross. Retreatants were encouraged to forsake many of life's legitimate pleasures. Some bishops banned the retreat in their jurisdictions, and some of those priests who preached it were sent to the hinterlands, including Lacouture and one of Dorothy's longtime spiritual directors, Fr. John Hugo.

Dorothy told of her meeting with Lacouture: "He was a very human, likable person. He laughed very joyously at some of the stories about some of our people who made the retreat and the extremes they went to." Still, she said, because of the retreat, "Our CW people began to see the thrilling reality of the spiritual life and began thinking in terms of their own lives. It paid lay people the compliment," she said, "of believing them to be capable of *growing* in the spiritual life." Then she summed up her gratitude for the retreat and those who led it: "I would say that it was about the best education I've had in the faith, and it was the teaching I expected when I became a Catholic."[14]

One of the most challenging aspects of the retreat was its apparent separation of the natural and the supernatural: that to grow in love of God and others, we must put aside not just actions and habits that are sinful or that might dull our sensibilities, but even some of the best and enjoyable things in life. This meant a strict self-discipline of one's desires, what in another context von Hügel called positively "a noble asceticism." It required a daily examination of one's conscience and a holding in check what St. Teresa of Ávila called the interior senses: the memory (not to remember past injuries, past worries), the understanding, and the will.

In von Hügel's *The Life of Prayer*, which Dorothy read often, she noted the comment of Fr. Frederick Faber concerning Ignatius Loyola's *Spiritual Exercises*: "This, then, my brethren, is St. Ignatius's way to heaven; and thank God, it is not the only way!"[15] Elsewhere, Dorothy underlined an observation of Abbot Columba Marmion: "Grace does not destroy nature. . . . Far from being opposed to one another, grace and nature, as regards what is good and pure in the latter, are in harmony, each preserving its own character and beauty."[16] She was able to bring this balance and maturity to the retreat; it saved her from falling prey to a false rigorism. At the end of one of her copies of *The Life of Prayer*, she wrote down a quote from Charles Williams's *Descent of the Dove*: "The rigorous view is necessary for sanctity; the relaxed for sanity."

When Dorothy wrote Cardinal Spellman in 1946 asking his support for a Catholic Worker retreat center on Staten Island, she acknowledged the need for such balance. "There has been a great deal of talk about the natural and the supernatural in Fr. Hugo's retreat," she informed the cardinal, "but one of our jobs as women is *to restore the natural*—the good natural." She then told him their Catholic Worker retreats always ended on a high note, with folk dancing, picnics, fish fries, discussions, and an emphasis on recreation. "We are trying to make [these] retreats for young people a taste of heaven."

Asked by a young Jesuit in 1972 whether his congregation should begin giving the Lacouture retreat again, Dorothy answered cautiously: "Different times require different things," she said. "I think you can't say what people should do. I think what was good for the forties may not be good for the seventies." But, she continued, there are always some "basic things that need to be emphasized," the chief being voluntary poverty. "You can never emphasize that enough, because it's a question of putting off the old man and putting on Christ."[17]

This putting on Christ, this taking up whatever cross or crosses one might be given—every day, perhaps many times a day—was at the heart of Dorothy's spirituality. She liked to quote St. Angela of Foligno that penances voluntarily undertaken are not half so meritorious as those imposed on us by the circumstances of our lives—and cheerfully borne. "Most of us have not the courage to set out on this path wholeheartedly," Dorothy said, "so God arranges it for us."[18]

Dorothy's life was rooted in prayer, for the distinct purpose of growing in love. "I cannot bear the [religious] romantics," she told Vivian Gornick of the *Village Voice* in a 1969 interview. "I want a religious realist. I want one who prays to see things as they are and to do something about it."[19] As she told Michael Cullen of the Milwaukee Catholic Worker the following year, she was convinced that prayer and austerity, prayer and self-sacrifice, prayer and fasting, prayer and protests were the indispensible means of creating a new society, but that these means were useless "unless animated by love."[20]

"Without prayer," Dorothy remarked in 1969, "we could not continue. As breath is to the body, prayer is to the soul."[21] The psalms were one of her daily portals to prayer. She quoted freely from them and highly recommended C. S. Lewis's *Reflections on the Psalms* (1958). It had been invaluable, she said, in coming to terms with the famous cursing psalms—the ones that gleefully damn one's enemies. (Lewis interpreted these, in part, to mean asking God's help to destroy our own inner demons.) A day without reading Scripture was a lost day, she said, for "the Word is so important, so beautiful, so comforting." In Edward J. Farrell's *Prayer Is a Hunger* (1972), she read that writing itself was a way into prayer, an opening to contemplation. "Writing can become a powerful way of prayer, a key to self-understanding and inner dialogue," Farrell wrote—and Dorothy underlined. She said she frequently wrote in church, and advised others on the staff of the paper to do so as well.

Von Hügel encouraged "much depth and breadth" in one's prayer life, "much variety and elasticity." He said the incarnational side of prayer must never be forgotten—meaning that each person must find the form of prayer God was calling one to—and recommended a "mixed *régime*," which for him included a decade of the rosary daily.[22] I remember driving with Dorothy one day to the Tivoli farm, north of New York City. She was at the wheel of her Volkswagen Bug, and we were deep in conversation when she nearly drove under a semi in front of us. She braked at the last moment, and then asked rather calmly and nonchalantly, "Shall we say the rosary?" It wasn't hard to say yes.

"The end and measure [of prayer] are the same," von Hügel wrote: "the love of God above all things and the love of our neighbor as ourselves." And "this love of God, where uninhibited and full," he continued, "brings joy."[23] One experienced that inner joy in Dorothy. It was as if the attention she paid to prayer permeated everything she did. "Often I find that I have started praying before I am really awake," she wrote in 1969, "just as I fall asleep praying 'Lord, Jesus, have mercy on us sinners,' over and over."[24]

CHAPTER SEVEN

Depression and the Duty of Delight

"The fullness of joy is to see God in all things." Dorothy had underlined this saying in Julian of Norwich's *Revelations of Divine Love*. Similarly, in her copy of Pope John XXIII's *Letters to His Family*, she had used a yellow marker to underscore Angelo Roncalli's advice (at the time he was papal nuncio to France) to a niece: "The worst malady of all is sadness, caused by lack of trust in the Lord, and the desire to impose our own will on him."

To overcome one's sadness or depressions, Dorothy advised "the duty of delight," a phrase of John Ruskin's. She quoted it in a conscious effort to lift her own spirits. For her that might mean going to the opera, reading a novel, visiting with old friends or listening to a concert on the radio. After hearing Brahms's Second Symphony one evening, she wrote: "joyful music to heal my sadness." All day, she noted, she had felt "oppressed in general by a sense of failure, a sense of sin."

Dorothy said that as a young person, her mother advised her to get up and clean the house when she got depressed.

She also mentioned that she had experienced several deep depressions. She said she had escaped them by "reading herself out of them"—in particular, by reading the novels of Dickens—but were she ever to experience such a depression again, she would want to have shock treatment. She warned her young coworkers not to get overworked or overwhelmed. As a young woman, she had attempted suicide as the result of a failed love affair. But when Kathleen and I knew her, that inclination seemed long over. Her empathy for others and her sense of the ominous nature of the times, did cause her sorrow, however, a sorrow you could glimpse in her eyes. But she did not pity people. As Bernanos observed, "the law of love is reciprocity, and reciprocity is not possible when there is pity." To pity someone is to sentimentalize them. Nor did Dorothy allow anyone to pity her.

Dorothy had an uncommon eye for finding beauty in the most forlorn of people and the sorriest of places. This ability did not arise simply from a need to escape her surroundings, but from a genuine appreciation for what she found there—what others (like me) habitually overlooked. She loved to quote Dostoyevsky that "beauty would save the world," and this was part of her application of the duty *to* delight. Indeed, you had to make choices when it came to "indulging the sense life," but the sense life was important because "it contributes a great deal to your life." She explained to an interviewer that the plays she had recently seen by Samuel Beckett "open your eyes to the sad beauty of the destitute that come to us." In making the effort to replenish your own spirit, you could then lift those of others. When fasting in Rome during Vatican II, she wrote a short prayer that concluded: "Give us, O Lord, peace, strength, and joy so that we in turn may give them to others."

Dorothy felt in sync with a recommendation Charles de Foucauld, the nineteenth-century explorer and mystic who lived among the Muslims of North Africa, had made to his sister: "There must be no economizing on good books." Dorothy's own library in her room was constantly being looted, freely borrowed from by others when she was away. Yet it was always replenished with other books people brought her. Her reading remained voracious and omnivorous to the end of her life: novels, drama, history, mystery, geology, biography, Scripture—and all the fields associated with them. Cardinal Spellman sent her an autographed copy of his novel; Thomas Merton provided a generous sampling of his works. She read Martin Buber and Hannah Arendt, and the economists R. H. Tawney and E. F. Schumacher. But it was the novels of Tolstoy and Dostoyevsky, Undset and Austen, Silone, Dickens, Conrad, and Greene to which she returned again and again—and encouraged others to read. It was as if she was hoping to inoculate the young Workers around her against sadness, depression, and burnout.

It was hope, finally, that Dorothy wished to inspire in others, and it was through her person that she did so. Quoting Peter Maurin, she told young Catholic Workers they should be "announcers, not denouncers." She herself set that tone in the paper and in person. Editorially, she followed Kropotkin's advice that "a revolutionary paper must be a record of those symptoms which everywhere announce the coming of a new era, the germination of new forms of social life." It is hope, he said, not despair that makes for successful change.

Still, Dorothy had no illusions that "a new heaven and a new earth" were about to arrive soon. "Our difficulties are not a transitory state of affairs," she had read and underlined in de Foucauld, "they are the normal state of affairs, and we shall reckon on being *in angustia temporum* all our lives so far as the good we want to do is concerned." This was "hope with a long view," coupled with a willingness to continue one's work even though it was not going to be harvested in one's lifetime.

For Dorothy, love sprang eternal. In October 1969 she wrote in her diary:

> I have fallen in love many a time in the fall of the year. I mean those times when body and soul are revived, and in the keen air of autumn after a hot, exhausting summer, I felt new strength to see, to "know" clearly, and to love, to look upon my neighbor and to love. Almost to be taken out of myself. I do not mean being in love with a particular person. I mean that quality of in-loveness that may brush like a sweet fragrance, a sound faintly heard, a sense of the beauty of one particular human being, or even one aspect of life. It may be an intuition of immortality, of the glory of God, of His Presence in the world. But it is almost impossible to put into words. The point is that it is general rather than particular, though it may come as a reminder, this flash of understanding, of recognition, with the reading of a particular book, or hearing some strain of music.
>
> It is tied up in some way also with the sense of hope, and an understanding of hope. How can we live without it, as a supernatural virtue, "hoping against hope," during this dark period of violence and suffering throughout the world?
>
> I am bold in trying to express the inexpressible, to write of happiness, even of Joy that comes, regardless of age, color, or condition of servitude to us all. Regardless of failures, regardless even of the sufferings of others. If we did not have this hope, this joy, this love, how could we help others? How could we have the strength to hold on to them, to hold them up when they are drowning in

sorrow, suffocating in blackness, almost letting go of life, life which we know with a sure knowledge is precious, which is something to hold to, be grateful for, to reverence.

This is the point of war protests, of a strong faith in the doctrine of nonviolence, the evidence of its continuing efficacy throughout the world.[1]

Late in life, Dorothy underscored in her copy of *Days of the Lord III* a quote from Søren Kierkegaard's *Fear and Trembling*: "Abraham believed and therefore he remained young, for he who always hopes for the best becomes old, deceived by life, and he who is always prepared for the worst grows old early, *but he who believes* preserves eternal youth."[2] She herself gave evidence of preserving such youth, and of praying to the end for what she called the primary virtues of fidelity and constancy.

CHAPTER EIGHT

A Personalist

What made Dorothy Day unique as well as inspiring? What makes her "approachable" for us today, despite her lifetime of prophetic witness and uncommon courage? Fundamentally, she was a personalist. She had an ideal of how important each person is, and in practice she approached each person as unique and revelatory of God's love. Her friend Ruth Collins said Dorothy wouldn't give anyone something to do without first putting that person in touch with another person who could help instruct him or her. "That was how my connection grew," Ruth said.

Dorothy's attention to others was the fruit of her hours of prayer. Her self-understanding issued from her daily self-examinations, made her aware of her own failings and need for God's grace. This culminated not only in acceptance of God's love for her, but in a growing, appreciative love for others. "Yes," she wrote in 1939 in *House of Hospitality*, "I see only too clearly how bad people are. I wish I did not see it. It is my own sins that give me such clarity."[1] As a result, she said, her daily prayer was that God might enlarge her heart "to see you all, and live with you all, in His love."

Her personalism was never simply a love for humanity, but for the mottled individual facing her, a person so like herself. This appreciation for others and their otherness was simply a manifestation of the thanksgiving she felt for God's all-surprising and insuperable love.

In public, Dorothy's personality was reticent. She had a keen intelligence that enabled her to intuit others' needs for delicacy and patience. On the other hand she could be a powerhouse, someone to be reckoned with and not one to let things drift. Nor did she suffer fools gladly. She could be brusque and on occasion hurtful. Still, she developed a sense of recognizing when this happened and, at least in her later years, would soon enough apologize to those she had hurt. These apologies were real, not self-excuses or a letting herself off the hook. There were times she knew she had gotten too much in the way of those who were trying to run the First Street House, and then she would simply pack up and leave for Tivoli the next day.

There was in Dorothy also a deep sense of modesty, coupled with her honesty and realism—first about herself, but also about what to expect, let alone demand, of others. In 1957 following her arrest for refusing to take shelter during the compulsory civil defense drills, she was given a thirty-day sentence in the Women's House of Detention in Greenwich Village (five days off for good behavior). She said she was looking forward to being in jail because then "*we* would not be running a house of hospitality" or ministering to the destitute, "but would truly be one of them."

Dorothy and her fellow women protesters were sent to the seventh floor of the jail. "We were surrounded," she wrote, "by a group of young women, colored and white, Puerto Rican and American, who first surveyed us boldly and then started making ribald comments." Dorothy was almost sixty at the time, but one of the young protesters jailed with her was Judith (Beck) Malina, whom Dorothy described as "young and beautiful," an actress "who carries herself consciously, alert to the gaze of others," and whose black hair hung down to her shoulders.

"Put her in my cell," yelled one of the roughest of the prisoners, clutching at Judith. "Let me have her," bellowed another. Then, Dorothy reported, "I had a great sinking of the heart, a great sense of terror for Judith." And with the urge to protect her, Dorothy *demanded*—her term—that Judith be put in her cell. "'I will make complaints,' I said firmly, 'if you do not do this.'" So the officer on duty put Judith in the cell with Dorothy. But that night, when the lights went out, Dorothy recalled, "we were stunned by the impact of our reception, and the wild, manic spirits of all those young women about us."[2]

"Jackie," the young woman who had groped for Judith, was released the following day. But within a week she had attempted suicide, and the *Daily News* reported, had been admitted to the Bellevue psychiatric prison ward. The following week she was again back in the House of Detention—but on a different floor from where Judith and Dorothy were still serving their sentences. All this made Dorothy reflect on her failure toward Jackie, her inability "to see that we are all brothers, we are all seeking love, seeking God." If only her love for Jackie had been stronger, Dorothy wrote, "casting out fear, I would not have taken a stand, I would have seen Christ in Jackie. Suppose Judith had been her cellmate for the night and been able to convey a little of the love the pacifists feel is the force which will overcome war. Perhaps, perhaps. . . ." But then Dorothy shifted perspectives again, challenging herself on a different level: "We can turn to our Lord Jesus Christ who has repaired already the greatest evil that ever happened, and trust that He will make up for our falls, for our neglects, for our failures in love."

Before her release, Dorothy told the other prisoners she would come back for a visit and that she would be outside to sing carols on Christmas Eve. Years later Garrick Beck—Judith and Julian Beck's son—wrote about tagging along with his folks as a boy to sing carols across the street from the jail. It was the first time he was exposed to Christianity and had to ask what the words meant, but he had a sense they were conveying something deep and beautiful to the women in the jail. About the fifth or sixth year, however, a woman in uniform emerged from the jail. Sporting a large set of keys as she crossed the street to approach the carolers, she spoke carefully, and even kindly. "I know you mean well," she said, "but you have no idea how upset you make the girls. They cry and cry after you are gone. You remind them of . . . their loved ones that they miss." Then she added, "If you care about these girls, let them get their rest." There followed, Garrick Beck recounted, "a moment as quiet as the twinkle of a star."

Then Dorothy Day stepped forward and began to address the warden. "In fact the very best Christmas present we could give these girls is some time with their families," Dorothy said. Then, leaning slightly closer to the officer, she went on, "You know, you could let these girls go home for Christmas. That would stop their crying. That's what Jesus would do if He had those keys." For a moment, Beck said, the warden made "a tiny smile at Dorothy," but then shook her head, backed up quickly, retraced her steps across the street, and reentered the jail—all the while shaking her head no. Garrick Beck returned each year to sing carols, until the jail was finally torn down in 1973. But what he remembered most vividly was Dorothy, "tall as the centuries, shimmering in the robe of bravery, gently, firmly speaking words that illuminate the way."

Relating to prisoners, prison officials, and other protesters was one thing, but how did Dorothy relate to members of her own Catholic Worker household? (As she told Vivian Gornick of the *Village Voice*, there "is an endless struggle among us. Not much Christian love here, I can tell you.")[3] The stories could be endless, and certainly endlessly entertaining. Here is just one, about a man nicknamed "Mad Paul." His real name was Paul Bruno, and he was around the New York Catholic Worker for decades. In her diary for 1963, Dorothy wrote concerning Paul:

> Paul used to work in the flower market up in the Thirties. . . . He is with us at least four years. He is Italian and he loves to cook, but with his irascible temper we only let him two nights a week. Every now and then he threatens people who irritate him, holding aloft a big meat cleaver.

> But every night he gathers together all the leavings on the plates of the eighty or so people who come to us for our evening meal and saves them in large cartons. . . . [Last] night Chuck Bassinetti [another CW regular] told me, he [Paul] takes the subway to the Pelham Bay station, gets out and walks two miles to a deserted part of the beach where he has built himself a little shack, and there he feeds the seagulls. . . . Then he . . . takes a dip in the sea, dries himself at a big fire of driftwood he has prepared, gets dressed again, and comes back to Chrystie St."

> "What? In this 20 degree weather?"

> "Yes, he does this winter and summer. I went with him once."

> The longing for beauty and space, light and moving water, the desire for healing, for well-being, that there is in these

men amongst whom we live for so many years and yet know so little.[4]

Some years after Dorothy's death, I was asked to go through papers in her room. I came upon a typed letter from Dorothy to Paul, written in 1974. It was in an envelope with Paul's name in Dorothy's hand. (My sense is that it may never have been delivered.)

Dear Paul,

It is some time since you wrote your letter to me, and the mail piles up so that I have not had time to answer it. But I just wanted you to know I do appreciate your help with the flowers you put around the cross, and the little statue of St. Joseph, and your love of cats, which I share with you, and your interest in recycling paper and cans and bottles. God bless you always for these examples you set us; and I know your patience is tried many times, as is my own, by all our trials and troublations, as John the farmer-seaman always says. Troubles everywhere, at the farm and here [at First St.] and among families and those who have no families. It is sharing the cross of Christ, and it is hard for each one of us to bear his own, and so hard too to be as sympathetic as we should be with those of others. Pray for me, Please, dear Paul, and God bless you always. Your fellow worker, Dorothy.

This brief note says a lot about how Dorothy approached others, in this case an irascible son of God. First there is appreciation for his singular contributions, minor though they might have seemed to some. Then follows encouragement and a subtle exhortation to greater patience by referring to the dignity of "sharing the cross of Christ." Then there is a sincere (and if you knew the man, humble) request for his prayers. Finally, there is the highest compliment, signing off, "Your fellow worker."

Dorothy had many lessons to share and many personalized means of responding to those who asked her advice. Still, she confessed, "I feel as though I fail people constantly—they come expecting to find a solution and there is no easy solution."

Jerry Ryan is, among other things, a fine spiritual writer and a translator of French theology into English. Before his arrest in Argentina in 1974 for opposing the military dictatorship there, he wrote a fine eye-witness account of the Pinochet coup d'état in Chile for the October–November 1973 *Catholic Worker*, under the pseudonym Jose Obrero. He first met Dorothy Day in 1958. He met her a second time in 1959, at the Catholic Worker farm in Rossville, Staten Island. A Josephite seminarian, he had become deeply impressed with the spirituality of Charles de Foucauld and was on his way to France to join the Little Brothers of Jesus. Passing through New York before saying good-bye to his family in Boston, he decided to look up Dorothy. (He had a ticket for a bus before dawn the following morning.) When he contacted the Worker in New York, Dorothy was not there. She was on Staten Island. He rang her up and was invited out for a visit.

It was a long trip, first by ferry and then across the length of the island. Ryan was met at the ferry house by a Catholic Worker, who drove him in a pickup truck to the farm. It was already sundown when they arrived, and it wasn't until everyone else had gone to bed that Ryan finally had a chance to talk with Dorothy.

They sat on an enclosed porch. "The conversation came easy, but I can't recall a word of what was said," Ryan recounted. "My only memories are of Dorothy calmly squashing a ferocious looking insect"—a June bug—and showing

Ryan a book she was reading and liking by Fulton J. Sheen. "When it occurred to me to look at my watch," Ryan said, it was three o'clock in the morning. "I told Dorothy that I had to start thinking about getting back to NYC in time to get my bus. I knew that first ferry left a bit after four." He thought Dorothy might wake up the fellow who had driven him out to the farm, but no such luck—she didn't want to disturb him. "Hitchhike," Dorothy offered.

"Well, I had no other choice," Ryan remembered. "We said good-bye and I stumbled out into a pitch-black night, hoping I could find the road and feeling like a perfect idiot trying to thumb a ride on a dirt road in the middle of no-where at half past three." He hadn't been there more than ten minutes, he said, "when a car showed up and took me to the ferry just in time." Ryan wrote later that the experience was something of a parable to him. "I was going off into the unknown [in France] and against all odds. It was as if Dorothy was showing me what could happen if only one trusted."

The journalist and feminist author Vivan Gornick had a different experience of Dorothy. Gornick had come to the First Street House to conduct an interview in 1969. First the two talked at one of the long tables in the kitchen where the soup line was served. Then they moved to the small backyard that Paul Bruno attended to. "I could feel," Gornick wrote in the *Village Voice*, "the truth of a love that categorically refused to deny the irreducible humanity in every talking creature." Suddenly, "the very human proportions of the daily grappling of Dorothy Day" became apparent to Gornick. At one point in their conversation, she felt that Dorothy had read her thoughts—and indeed she had, Gornick wrote—but, she continued, Dorothy's words "were meant not to rebuke me, but to soothe me; and, indeed, I felt eased."

Gornick concluded that she found in Dorothy "a woman who had done many things she would wish not to have done," and who had "been alone a long, long time in a curious, exalted, exhausting manner." More important, none of it was "a comfortable matter of the past; all of this was an ongoing affair." Gornick recognized Dorothy's faith as being put through the fire daily, and that her relation to Christ had "become a tempered, disciplined, ritualized business."[5]

When Dorothy was asked several years later why she was so taken with Pietro Spina, Ignazio Silone's hero in *Bread and Wine*, she said it was because Spina had the courage to write "No" on a wall, denouncing the Fascists who ran Italy. "One person shouting 'No' is enough to break the unanimity," Dorothy said. "I thought that was the most beautiful thing to say. That's the personalist approach."[6]

CHAPTER NINE

Sainthood?

For those who knew Dorothy Day, there is no doubt she was and is a saint. Miracles needed to commend canonization have already been witnessed: the singularity of her life; the good and prophetic works she performed and suffered for; the multiplication of loaves and fishes that continues at Catholic Worker houses around the world decades after her death and that encourages other groups and parishes to "go and do likewise"; and the ongoing witness for peace and justice that she inspired in countless individuals and communities. Dorothy exemplified what Pope Benedict XVI reminded Catholics in *Deus Caritas Est* (28): "The church cannot and must not remain on the sidelines in the fight for justice."

Unlike plaster saints, real saints—the only ones that count—are sinners like ourselves, flesh and blood, who manage to incarnate in one or another aspect of their lives the living Christ. It is for this reason we honor them, learn from them, wish to emulate them, and want to be with them.

Dorothy was a complex, compelling, and sometimes contradictory person. She was in many respects "disarming."

There was in her a purity of soul that helped one glimpse God's purity, and an acceptance of simplicity that helped one appreciate each morsel eaten. The New York poet and educator Ned O'Gorman once described her as one of the most sophisticated, self-possessed, and beautiful women he ever met. "There was in her a radiant, transcendent authenticity," he said.[1] There was also a radicalness that made you want to share the sufferings of others and to change the world; a love of beauty, music, and song that could lift your heart when you were with her; and the steady purposefulness of her walk that gave you a new liveliness as you progressed down the block with her.

In 1997 the historian Patrick Allitt wrote in a *New York Times* op-ed on the centennial of Dorothy's birth that she was simply "too interesting to be a saint." He hoped that she would not be declared one since, he said, "it would flatten out her complex, spiky personality, coating it with a gloss of holiness," and—particularly important to him, a historian—"lift her out of her unique historical situation."[2]

I don't think this is so. Even in her own lifetime, people recognized Dorothy's "spiky saintliness." A bartender was once overheard expounding on it. "She's a saint," he said. This was in the 1930s, not that long after the Catholic Worker was started. And the person who overheard this remark, I am told, was one of Dorothy's nearest and most severe critics: her father.

Twenty-plus years before Dorothy's death, John Cogley wrote in *Commonweal* that "she is a great woman, the very greatest that we [American Catholics] have. Historians will take the measure of American Catholicism, I suspect, by measuring our attitude toward her."[3] Dorothy's radical assumption—and it seems even more radical today—was that we are all made in God's image and likeness. We are conceived out of God's love, and we all matter; matter itself matters; and all matter is holy. In *The Discovery of God* (1956), Henri de Lubac wrote that the most distressing diagnosis that can be made of the present age is that—and Dorothy had underlined this—"it has lost its taste for God."[4]

Peter Maurin had described secularism as "a separation of the spiritual and the material." So when Communists would invite Dorothy to talk—and this happened especially during the Popular Front years of 1935–39 and 1941–45—she would often short circuit the conversation by simply reminding them "Lenin said that atheism is an integral part of Marxism." When speaking at Carnegie Hall in 1952 during the McCarthy era, she told her audience that she was doing so precisely as a Catholic believer: "To many who are listening here tonight, the injection of these religious truths into the discussion may not seem relevant, but they are the reason I am here." Dorothy forced materialists, secularists, and even her own father, to reexamine themselves.

Dorothy liked to quote Charles Péguy that the reason we have so few saints is because we have not asked for them. Without the saints, Péguy's fellow Frenchman Georges Bernanos wrote, "Christianity would long since have become a gigantic heap of ruins." In that spirit, Dorothy wrote for Helene Iswolsky's *The Third Hour* in 1949: "We are all called to be saints, and we might as well get over our bourgeois fear of that name." Further, she told her friend Mary Lathrop, Maurin taught that what is needed today is a host of uncanonized saints, and that we should all strive to be included in *that* number.

In her 1964 diary Dorothy noted that St. Thérèse of Lisieux—one of her "top-drawer" favorites—"wrote that if the Lord could pick out anyone less than herself to make a saint he would have done so."[5] I think Dorothy quoted the line because she felt it applied to herself. "Few people, few Christians," John Cort observed in 2003 (he had known Dorothy since 1936 when he joined the *Catholic Worker* as a young reporter), had demonstrated the ability to continue living out the precepts of Matthew 25:32-46 (feed the hungry, clothe the naked, etc.) "as she did for so many years." She was able to do it, Cort was convinced, "because she, in fact could see the face of Christ in the least, the poorest, the most desolate and unattractive of our brothers and sisters."[6] It was her gift, her message, and her example. When Daniel Berrigan, SJ, was asked if Dorothy should be canonized, he was cautious: "We have here a saint whose soul ought not be stolen from her people—the wretched of the earth."[7]

Before Nina Polcyn Moore's death in 2007 (she was one of Dorothy's longest and dearest friends), she sent me some materials related to Dorothy. They included a page from a recently published catechetical text for intermediate or high school students. (Nina had attended the meetings with Cardinal John O'Connor that had led him to initiate Dorothy's canonization process in 2000.) The page from the catechetical text included an illustration of Dorothy, looking like a 1980s nun in matching blue uniform and head scarf. The accompanying text concentrated on Dorothy's preconversion love life: her abortion, rebound marriage, and divorce, and even dissected her common-law husband, the father of her daughter, as "a botanist and a heavy drinker." (The origin of this unattributed latter factoid remains a mystery. Dorothy never spoke about Forster that way, and he seemed to have no such proclivities when you were with him.) But Nina's response was telling—and perhaps she was voicing her misgivings about the canonization process in general: "They are all going to crucify Dorothy in their own way," she said.

When Frank Donovan, Dorothy's closest aide during her final decade, was asked by a reporter what she meant by her famous dismissal, "Don't call me a saint," he replied: "She was saying, 'I'm proposing things to you, and I want you to listen and try to change your life so you can help other people change theirs.'" Then, Frank added, "She said, 'Don't call me a saint'; she didn't say, 'Don't ever call me a saint.' She was not rejecting the concept of sainthood."[8]

I think Dorothy was more than simply a saint, however. Nina Polcyn Moore told Cardinal O'Connor she thought Dorothy ought to be declared a doctor of the church. Coming from Nina—who helped found the original Catholic Worker house in Milwaukee, ran a Catholic book center in Chicago for decades, and was deeply immersed in theology and the writings of the church doctors—it was a suggestion demanding respect. Yet my own sense of Dorothy differs a bit: she is a prophet, an American prophet, who called not only individuals, but the church, the state, and American society itself to account. There must be a closing of the gap between private and public morality, Dorothy taught, and questioned both our materialism and militarism. "What is worst of all," she wrote in 1961, "is *using* God and religion to bolster up our own greed, our own attachment to property, and putting God and country on an equality."[9] Further, in this land where happiness is viewed as a constitutional right, there must be a new willingness to encounter Christ in others and on the cross. In his *Prophetic Jesus, Prophetic Church* (2011), theologian Luke Timothy Johnson writes that "prophecy is not merely a matter of words spoken, but a way of being in the world; it brings God's will into human history through words, yes, but also the deeds and character of the prophet."[10] *New York Times* columnist Peter Steinfels once described Dorothy as a "minister of restlessness." She was, he said, someone who kept pushing us—even the multitudes of people like himself "who might never accept her total pacifism or her communitarian anarchism."[11]

Dean Brackley, SJ, once asked Dorothy if she thought the Jesuits should corporately commit themselves to pacifism. "I don't believe in corporately committing yourself to anything," she responded. "I mean it is a question of vocation." And then, she followed, "I have very strong feelings about vocation. It doesn't all have to be the same thing." She wasn't expecting Brackley, for example, to live on the Bowery, doing the work of the Catholic Worker (although he lived nearby at the time and was assisting poor children at the neighborhood Nativity Mission school center). "I think that people have different vocations and that the thing to do is to ask God to show us what it is. And once we find it, we follow it." After that, it was a matter of "Do what you are doing."[12]

Paradoxically, this might mean doing almost nothing visibly noteworthy. In encouraging Thomas Merton to remain steadfast in his vocation, Dorothy told him (it was the year before his death) "the thing I love about the Little Brothers of Jesus is they really know how to do nothing." She had just visited their community in Detroit, where they worked and lived among the poor, emulating the "hidden life" of Jesus at Nazareth. "What a tremendous amount can be accomplished by just doing nothing," she told Merton. And, the older she got, the more she stressed that faithfulness and perseverance "are the greatest virtues—accepting a sense of failure we all must have in our work, in the work of others around us, since Christ was the world's greatest failure." She called such failure "the pattern of the cross," but reiterated that "in the cross is joy of spirit." At the age of seventy-seven she wrote, "Here I am . . . trying to grow in the life of the spirit. I feel that I am but a beginner." Still, she said, her strength returned to her each day "with a cup of coffee and the reading of the psalms."[13]

In the Hasidic tradition—one Dorothy held in great esteem—a *zaddik* is a righteous person who has stood the test and been proven. In 1972 a small Hasidic synagogue in Manhattan presented her with its Baal Shem Tov Award, named for Hasidism's founder, and declared her "A Woman of Valor." For Dorothy, it was never a matter of seeking awards or public recognition, but only maintaining her "sense of the necessity of keeping our own integrity."[14] We can only try to change ourselves, first of all. While she recommended the study of history and of the lives of great women and men, the whole point was to realize that "we begin with ourselves."[15]

Some people, Dorothy opined in her 1961 diary, "think the most important task of the Catholic Worker is peace—to clarify thought about modern war, man's freedom, and the use of force; other people go deeper and say voluntary 'poverty' is the answer; others say 'providence.' But truly, 'Love' is the reason for it all. 'Love your enemies, do good to those who hate you, bless those who curse you. . . . Give to him who asks of thee, and from him who takes away thy goods, ask no return.' "[16] She acknowledged that it is sobering to realize we love God as much as we love the one we love least.

Love, St. Bernard wrote (Sermon 83), is sufficient of itself: "It is its own merit, its own reward; its profit lies in its practice." And in *The Brothers Karamazov*, Fr. Zosima famously advised his followers that "love in action is a harsh and dreadful thing, compared to love in dreams." There will inevitably be a "costingness" to it, as von Hügel noted. Love, nevertheless, engenders joy, and is its own reward and renewal.

No wonder those who knew Dorothy Day came away enlivened but shaken. "To have known Dorothy means spending the rest of your life wondering what hit you," her granddaughter Kate wrote seventeen years after Dorothy's death. "On the one hand, she has given so many of us a home, physically and spiritually; on the other, she has shaken our very foundations."[17]

At the time of her death, J. M. Cameron memorialized Dorothy in the *New York Review of Books*. Her "prose matched her spiritual purity," Cameron wrote. "The style, the integrity, the magnanimity, the beauty of Dorothy Day's work and character will be remembered when many of those who made greater noise in their day are quite forgotten."[18]

Amen, and *Deo gratias*.

Notes

Introduction—pages 1–12

1. See *All the Way to Heaven: The Selected Letters of Dorothy Day*, ed. Robert Ellsberg (Milwaukee: Marquette University Press, 2010), 397.

2. Interview with author, February 2008. See Patrick Jordan, "Ready for Whatever Happens," *Catholic Worker* (May 2008): 2.

3. Thomas Goekler, "Maryknoll Priest Remembers Dorothy Day," *Houston Catholic Worker* (November–December 2008): 4.

4. See "Elizabeth Gurley Flynn: Red Roses for Her," in *Dorothy Day: Selected Writings*, ed. Robert Ellsberg (Maryknoll, NY: Orbis, 1992), 145.

5. See Rosalie G. Riegle, *Dorothy Day: Portraits by Those Who Knew Her* (Maryknoll, NY: Orbis, 2003), 120. Used with the permission of James Douglass.

6. Doug Lavine, "Dorothy Day: 40 Years of Works of Mercy," *National Catholic Reporter* (June 8, 1973): 7.

7. From a yet-to-be-published manuscript, quoted here with the author's permission.

8. Gerard E. Sherry, "'Jail Is Almost Like a Motel' to 75-Year-Old Dorothy Day," *National Catholic Reporter* (August 17, 1973): 1.

9. John C. Cort, *Dreadful Conversions* (New York: Fordham University Press, 2003), 30.

10. Jim Forest, *All Is Grace: A Biography of Dorothy Day* (Maryknoll, NY: Orbis, 2011), 45.

Chapter One:
A Chronology—pages 13–28

1. Jim Forest, *All Is Grace: A Biography of Dorothy Day* (Maryknoll, NY: Orbis, 2011), 138.

2. "Notes for a Conference [1953]," in *The Duty of Delight: The Diaries of Dorothy Day*, ed. Robert Ellsberg (Milwaukee: Marquette University Press, 2008), 184.

3. *The Habit of Being: Letters of Flannery O'Connor*, ed. Sally Fitzgerald (New York: Farrar, Straus, Giroux, 1979), 218.

Chapter Two:
Radical Roots, Molecular Moral Forces—
pages 29–36

1. Elie Wiesel, *Souls on Fire* (New York: Random House, 1972), 19, 21.

2. Nicholas von Hoffmann, "A Saint for the Times: New York's Dorothy Day," *The New York Observer* (December 29, 1997): 4.

3. Garry Wills, "Dorothy Day at the Barricades," *Esquire* (December 1983): 228.

4. William F. Buckley Jr., "A Gift Returned" *National Review* (November 29, 1985): 54. In November 1997, Senate Resolution 163 designated a National Week of Recognition for Dorothy Day and Those Whom She Served. Further, on September 24, 2015, Pope Francis reminded a joint session of Congress of the important contribution that Servant of God Dorothy Day made to American history.

5. See "Aims and Purposes," *Catholic Worker* (February 1940): 7.

6. Martin Buber, *Paths in Utopia* (Boston: Beacon, 1958), 43.

7. George P. Carlin, letter to the author, October 22, 1997.

8. See *Catholic Worker* (March–April 1973): 6; *The Letters of William James*, vol. II, ed. Henry James (Boston: Atlantic Monthly, 1920), 90.

Chapter Three:
Conversions—pages 37–49

1. See Dorothy Day, *The Long Loneliness* (New York: Harper and Row, 1952), 119.

2. Ibid., 236.

3. Patrick Kavanagh, *The Great Hunger* (Dublin: Cuala, 1942).

4. Day, "Pilgrimage to Mexico," *Commonweal* (December 26, 1958): 336.

5. Day, "Michael Gold," *Catholic Worker* (June 1967): 2.

6. Luke Timothy Johnson, "Human & Divine: Did Jesus Have Faith?" *Commonweal* (January 31, 2008): 16.

7. Day, "The Brother and the Rooster," *Dorothy Day: Writings from Commonweal*, ed. Patrick Jordan (Collegeville, MN: Liturgical Press, 2002), 1–6.

8. Dwight Macdonald, "Profiles: The Foolish Things of the World—1," *New Yorker* (October 4, 1952): 37.

9. Peter Maurin, *The Green Revolution: Easy Essays on Catholic Radicalism* (Fresno, CA: Academy Guild Press, 1961), 77.

10. Peter Maurin, *Catholic Radicalism* (New York: Catholic Worker Books, 1949), 49.

11. Maurin, *The Green Revolution*, 110–11.

12. Ibid., 116–17.

13. Dom Luigi Sturzo, *Church and State*, reissued (Notre Dame, IN: University of Notre Dame Press, 1962), 27.

14. Ida Friederike Görres, *The Hidden Face: A Study of St. Thérèse of Lisieux* (New York: Pantheon, 1959), 229.

15. Day, "Tobacco Road," *Commonweal* (November 26, 1943), 140.

16. Pontifical Council for Justice and Peace, *Compendium of the Social Doctrine of the Church* (Libreria Editrice Vaticana, 2005), 19.

Chapter Four:
Principles and Convergences—pages 50–65

1. Introduction, *Two Agitators: Peter Maurin—Ammon Hennacy* (New York: Catholic Worker, 1959), 2.

2. See Dorothy Day, *Loaves and Fishes* (New York: Harper and Row, 1963), 161.

3. Day, "Poverty Is to Care and Not to Care," *Catholic Worker* (April 1953): 5.

4. See Day, *On Pilgrimage* (New York: Catholic Worker Books, 1948), 102.

5. *The Duty of Delight: The Diaries of Dorothy Day*, ed. Robert Ellsberg (Milwaukee: Marquette University Press, 2008), 113.

6. Day, "On Pilgrimage," *Catholic Worker* (March 1948): 2.

7. Day, *The Long Loneliness* (New York: Harper and Row, 1952), 45.

8. See Patrick Jordan, "Helder Camara—Bishop of Development," *Catholic Worker* (May 1970): 8.

9. Day, Letter, *Commonweal* (November 3, 1939): 59.

10. Day, "The Scandal of the Works of Mercy," *Commonweal* (November 4, 1949): 99.

11. Ibid., 100–101

12. See Kassie Temple, "Peter Maurin: Shaking the Foundations of Modernity," *Catholic Worker* (May 1989): 5.

13. Day, "On Pilgrimage," *Catholic Worker* (December 1969): 5.

14. See Dean Brackley and Dennis Dillon, "An Interview with Dorothy Day," *National Jesuit News* (May 1972): 10.

15. "We Go on Record," *Catholic Worker* (September 1945): 1.

16. Day, "On Pilgrimage," *Catholic Worker* (February 1969): 5.

17. *All the Way to Heaven: The Selected Letters of Dorothy Day*, ed. Robert Ellsberg (Milwaukee: Marquette University Press, 2010), 384.

18. Jim Wallis and Wes Michaelson, "Dorothy Day: Exalting Those in Low Degree," *Sojourners* (December 1976): 18.

19. *Two Agitators*, 2.

20. Day, "CW Refuses Tax Exemption," *Catholic Worker* (May 1972): 3.

21. Author's notes, meeting on June 26, 1972.

22. Day, "On Pilgrimage," *Catholic Worker* (July–August 1972): 2.

23. See *Days of the Lord III*, ed. William G. Storey (New York: Herder & Herder, 1969), 140, 141.

Chapter Five:
Catholicity and Lady Poverty—pages 66–80

1. Dorothy Day, *On Pilgrimage: The Sixties* (New York: Curtis Books, 1972), 18.

2. Charles Péguy, *Basic Verities* (New York: Pantheon, 1943), 179.

3. Rosemary Haughton, *The Catholic Thing* (Springfield, IL: Templegate, 1979), 55.

4. Dorothy Day, mimeographed remarks, "Fear in Our Time," October 1963, Spode House Conference of Pax, 14. See also Day, "On Pilgrimage," *Catholic Worker* (November 1963): 6.

5. Day, "The Case of Cardinal McIntyre," *Catholic Worker* (July–August 1964): 8.

6. Day, Letter to Msgr. Edward Gaffney, January 28, 1951. See *All the Way to Heaven: The Selected Letters of Dorothy Day*, ed. Robert Ellsberg (Milwaukee: Marquette University Press, 2010), 191.

7. Ammon Hennacy, *The One-Man Revolution in America* (Salt Lake City: Ammon Hennacy Publications, 1970), 331.

8. Day, Letter of October 29, 1968. See *All the Way to Heaven*, 351.

9. Day, *House of Hospitality* (New York: Sheed and Ward, 1939), 266–67.

10. Kate Hennessy, statement prepared for a meeting for the Cause of Dorothy Day, New York Catholic Center, June 7, 2005, emailed copy to author.

11. Dean Brackley and Dennis Dillon, "An Interview with Dorothy Day," *National Jesuit News* (May 1972): 10.

12. Jeff Dietrich, "Dorothy Day—Not Your Everyday Saint," *Catholic Agitator* (December 1971, reprinted June 2000): 4.

13. Day, "On Pilgrimage," *Catholic Worker* (November 1967): 7.

14. Day, "In Peace Is My Bitterness Most Bitter," *Catholic Worker* (January 1967): 2.

15. Day, "On Pilgrimage," *Catholic Worker* (March 1960): 6.

16. Day, "Southern Pilgrimage," *Commonweal* (March 31, 1962): 11.

17. Gerard E. Sherry, "'Jail Is Almost Like a Motel' to 75-Year-Old Dorothy Day," *National Catholic Reporter* (August 17, 1973): 17.

18. Day, *On Pilgrimage: The Sixties*, 331.

19. Day, "On Pilgrimage," *Catholic Worker* (July–August 1962): 7.

20. Day, "On Pilgrimage," *Catholic Worker* (September 1964): 8.

21. Day, Letter to Karl Meyer of August 13, 1971, *All the Way to Heaven*, 331.

22. Day, *The Duty of Delight: The Diaries of Dorothy Day*, ed. Robert Ellsberg (Milwaukee: Marquette University Press, 2008), 315.

23. Day, "Funds Needed to Carry On Work in N.Y.," *Catholic Worker* (September 1939): 1.

24. Kate Hennessy, "Memories of Compassion and Abundant Love," *Catholic Worker* (October–November 1997): 1.

25. Day, Appeal Letter, October 1957.

26. Day, "The Case of Cardinal McIntyre," 8.

27. Day, *On Pilgrimage: The Sixties*, 361.

28. Day, "The Mystery of the Poor," *Catholic Worker* (April 1964): 8.

29. See *The Dorothy Day Book*, ed. Margaret Quigley and Michael Garvey (Springfield, IL: Templegate, 1982), 18.

30. *Regula Pastoralis*, 3:21: PL 77, 87. See Pontifical Council for Justice and Peace, *Compendium of the Social Doctrine of the Church* (Libreria Editrice Vaticana, 2005), 80.

31. See John C. Cort, *Dreadful Conversions* (New York: Fordham University Press, 2003), 34.

32. John Cogley, "Dorothy Day, Comforter," *New York Times* (November 8, 1972): 47.

33. Day, "On Pilgrimage," *Catholic Worker* (December 1961): 7.

Chapter Six:
Peace and the Primacy of the Spiritual—
pages 81–89

1. Dorothy Day, "On Pilgrimage," *Catholic Worker* (March–April 1975): 2.

2. Day, *On Pilgrimage: The Sixties* (New York: Curtis Books, 1972), 21.

3. Day, "On Pilgrimage," *Catholic Worker* (February 1960): 2.

4. See Dorothy Day, Catholic Worker Collection, Marquette University Archives, Series W-6.4, Box 1, Folder 7 (Civil Defense Protests folder).

5. Day, Letter in *All the Way to Heaven: The Selected Letters of Dorothy Day*, ed. Robert Ellsberg (Milwaukee: Marquette University Press, 2010), 367.

6. John Cogley, "The Catholic Worker," *Commonweal* (May 16, 1958), 180.

7. Doug Lavine, "Dorothy Day: 40 Years of Works of Mercy," *National Catholic Reporter* (June 8, 1973): 17.

8. See Joseph Cunneen, "The Films of Robert Bresson," *Commonweal* (February 9, 2001): 113.

9. See "Aims and Purposes," *Catholic Worker* (February 1940): 7.

10. See John C. Cort, "In a Time of Gigantic Evil," *Commonweal* (September 24, 1982): 502.

11. Day, "On Pilgrimage," *Catholic Worker* (June 1972): 7.

12. See *The Duty of Delight: The Diaries of Dorothy Day*, ed. Robert Ellsberg (Milwaukee: Marquette University Press, 2008), 37.

13. See Day, "On Pilgrimage," *Catholic Worker* (January 1962): 1.

14. Dean Brackley and Dennis Dillon, "An Interview with Dorothy Day," *National Jesuit News* (May 1972): 8.

15. Baron Friedrich von Hügel, *The Life of Prayer* (New York: E. P. Dutton, 1929), 40.

16. See *Days of the Lord II*, ed. William G. Storey (New York: Herder & Herder, 1966), 6.

17. Brackley and Dillon, "Interview," 8.

18. Day, "On Pilgrimage," *Catholic Worker*, January 1948, in *Dorothy Day: Selected Writings* (Maryknoll, NY: Orbis, 1992), 208.

19. Vivian Gornick, "Dorothy Day at 72: The Dailiness of Grace," *Village Voice* (November 20, 1969): 6.

20. Day, Letter, ca. February 1970, in *All the Way to Heaven*, 367.

21. See July 9, 1969, *The Duty of Delight*, 458.

22. Von Hügel, *The Life of Prayer*, 25, 45.

23. Ibid., 61.

24. See February 4, 1969, *The Duty of Delight*, 436.

Chapter Seven:
Depression and the Duty of Delight—pages 90–94

1. See *The Duty of Delight: The Diaries of Dorothy Day*, ed. Robert Ellsberg (Milwaukee: Marquette University Press, 2008), 464–65.

2. See *Days of the Lord III*, ed. William G. Storey (New York: Herder & Herder, 1969), 60.

Chapter Eight: A Personalist—pages 95–103

1. See *Dorothy Day: Selected Writings*, ed. Robert Ellsberg (Maryknoll, NY: Orbis, 1992), 88.

2. Day, "We Plead Guilty," *Commonweal* (December 27, 1957): 331.

3. Vivian Gornick, "Dorothy Day at 72: The Dailiness of Grace," *Village Voice* (November 20, 1969): 31.

4. See December 14, 1963, *The Duty of Delight: The Diaries of Dorothy Day*, ed. Robert Ellsberg (Milwaukee: Marquette University Press, 2008), 344.

5. Gornick, "Dorothy Day at 72," 5, 6, 31, 32.

6. See Jim Wallis and Wes Michaelson, "Dorothy Day: Exalting Those in Low Degree," *Sojourners* (December 1976): 18.

Chapter Nine: Sainthood?—pages 104–11

1. See Rosalie Riegle, *Dorothy Day: Portraits by Those Who Knew Her* (Maryknoll, NY: Orbis, 2003), 123.

2. Patrick Allitt, "Too Interesting to Be a Saint," *New York Times* (November 15, 1997): A 17.

3. John Cogley, "The Catholic Worker," *Commonweal* (May 16, 1958): 180.

4. See *Days of the Lord II*, ed. William G. Storey (New York: Herder & Herder, 1966), 72.

5. See September 18, 1964, *The Duty of Delight: The Diaries of Dorothy Day*, ed. Robert Ellsberg (Milwaukee: Marquette University Press, 2008), 351.

6. See John C. Cort, *Dreadful Conversions* (New York: Fordham University Press, 2003), 22.

7. See T. Wright Townsend, "The Reluctant Saint," *Chicago Tribune Magazine* (December 26, 1999): 15.

8. Ibid., 15.

9. Dorothy Day, "About Cuba," *Catholic Worker* (July–August 1961): 8.

10. Luke Timothy Johnson, *Prophetic Jesus, Prophetic Church* (Grand Rapids, MI: Eerdmans, 2011), 41.

11. Peter Steinfels, "Beliefs" Column, *New York Times* (November 15, 1997): A 14.

12. Dean Brackley and Dennis Dillon, "An Interview with Dorothy Day," *National Jesuit News* (May 1972): 9, 10.

13. See *Dorothy Day: Selected Writings*, ed. Robert Ellsberg (Maryknoll, NY: Orbis, 1992), 353.

14. See February 24, 1940, *The Duty of Delight*, 52.

15. See September 24, 1968, ibid., 427.

16. See February 24, 1961, ibid., 310.

17. Kate Hennessy, "Memories of Compassion and Abundant Love," *Catholic Worker* (October–November 1997): 1.

18. J. M. Cameron, "Dorothy Day (1897–1980)," *New York Review of Books* (January 22, 1981): 8.

Bibliography

Primary Sources

Day, Dorothy. *All the Way to Heaven: The Selected Letters of Dorothy Day*. Edited by Robert Ellsberg. Milwaukee: Marquette University Press, 2010.

———. *By Little and by Little: Selected Writings of Dorothy Day*. Edited by Robert Ellsberg. New York: Alfred A. Knopf, 1983. Reissued as *Dorothy Day: Selected Writings*. Maryknoll, NY: Orbis Books, 1992.

———. *The Duty of Delight: The Diaries of Dorothy Day*. Edited by Robert Ellsberg. Milwaukee: Marquette University Press, 2008.

———. *From Union Square to Rome*. Silver Spring, MD: Preservation of the Faith Press, 1938. Reissued by Orbis Books, 2006.

———. *House of Hospitality*. New York: Sheed & Ward, 1939. Reissued by Our Sunday Visitor, 2015.

———. *Loaves and Fishes*. New York: Harper & Row, 1963. Reissued by Orbis Books, 1997.

———. *The Long Loneliness*. New York: Harper & Row, 1952. Reissued by HarperSanFrancisco, 1980.

———. *Meditations*. Selected and arranged by Stanley Vishnewski. New York: Newman Press, 1970.

———. *On Pilgrimage*. New York: Catholic Worker Books, 1948. Reissued by William B. Eerdmans Publishing, 1999.

————. *On Pilgrimage: The Sixties*. New York: Curtis Books, 1972.

————. *Peter Maurin: Apostle to the World*. With Francis J. Sicius. Maryknoll, NY: Orbis Books, 2004.

————. *Therese*. Notre Dame, IN: Fides Publishers Association, 1960. Reissued by Templegate Publishers, 1979.

————. *Writings from Commonweal*. Edited by Patrick Jordan. Collegeville, MN: Liturgical Press, 2002.

Many of Dorothy Day's writings can be accessed online at www.catholicworker.org/dorothyday.

Maurin, Peter. *The Green Revolution*. 2nd rev. ed. Fresno, CA: Academy Guild Press, 1961.

Peter Maurin's Easy Essays can be accessed online at www.catholicworker.org/petermaurin.

Secondary Sources

Brackley, Dean, and Dennis Dillon. "An Interview with Dorothy Day." *National Jesuit News* (May 1972): 8–10.

Coles, Robert. *Dorothy Day: A Radical Devotion*. Reading, MA: Addison-Wesley, 1987.

————. *A Spectacle unto the World*. With photographs by Jon Erikson. New York: The Viking Press, 1973.

Cook, Jack. *Bowery Blues: A Tribute to Dorothy Day*. Bloomington, IN: Xlibris, 2001.

Cornell, Thomas C., Robert Ellsberg, and Jim Forest, eds. *A Penny a Copy: Readings from The Catholic Worker*. Maryknoll, NY: Orbis Books, 1995.

Cort, John C. *Dreadful Conversions: The Making of a Catholic Socialist*. New York: Fordham University Press, 2003.

Coy, Patrick, ed. *A Revolution of the Heart*. Philadelphia: Temple University Press, 1988.

d'Entremont, Nicole. *City of Belief: A Novel*. Peaks Island, ME: Fox Print Books, 2009.

Elie, Paul. *The Life You Save May Be Your Own: An American Pilgrimage*. New York: Farrar, Straus & Giroux, 2003.

Forest, Jim. *All Is Grace: A Biography of Dorothy Day*. Maryknoll, NY: Orbis Books, 2011.

Haughton, Rosemary. *The Catholic Thing*. Springfield, IL: Templegate Publishers, 1979.

Hennacy, Ammon. *The One-Man Revolution in America*. Salt Lake City: Ammon Hennacy Publications, 1970.

Iswolsky, Helene. *No Time to Grieve: An Autobiographical Journey*. Philadelphia: The Winchell Company, 1985.

Klejment, Anne, and Nancy L. Roberts, eds. *American Catholic Pacifism: The Influence of Dorothy Day and the Catholic Worker Movement*. Westport, CT: Praeger, 1996.

Larson, Claudia. *Don't Call Me a Saint*. DVD. dorothydaydoc .com. One Lucky Dog Productions, 2007.

McGrath, Michael O'Neill. *Saved by Beauty: A Spiritual Journey with Dorothy Day*. Franklin Park, IL: World Library Publications, 2012.

McGreevy, John T. *Catholicism and American Freedom: A History*. New York: W.W. Norton, 2003.

Merriman, Brigid O'Shea. *Searching for Christ: The Spirituality of Dorothy Day*. Notre Dame, IN: University of Notre Dame Press, 1994.

Miller, William D. *All Is Grace: The Spirituality of Dorothy Day*. Garden City, NY: Doubleday, 1987.

———. *Dorothy Day: A Biography*. San Francisco: Harper & Row, 1982.

———. *A Harsh and Dreadful Love: Dorothy Day and the Catholic Worker Movement*. New York: Liveright, 1973.

Morris, Charles R. *American Catholic: The Saints and Sinners Who Built America's Most Powerful Church*. New York: Vintage Books, 1998.

O'Brien, David J. *American Catholics and Social Reform*. New York: Oxford University Press, 1968.

O'Grady, Jim. *Dorothy Day: With Love for the Poor*. Staten Island, NY: Ward Hill Press, 1993.

Piehl, Mel. *Breaking Bread: The Catholic Worker and the Origin of Catholic Radicalism in America*. Philadelphia: Temple University Press, 1982.

Quigley, Margaret, and Michael Garvey, eds. *The Dorothy Day Book*. Springfield, IL: Templegate Publishers, 1982.

Riegle, Rosalie G. *Dorothy Day: Portraits by Those Who Knew Her*. Maryknoll, NY: Orbis Books, 2003.

Roberts, Nancy. *Dorothy Day and The Catholic Worker*. Albany: State University of New York Press, 1984.

Thorn, William, Philip Runkel, and Susan Mountain, eds. *Dorothy Day and the Catholic Worker Movement: Centenary Essays*. Milwaukee: Marquette University Press, 2001.

Troester, Rosalie Riegle, comp. and ed. *Voices from the Catholic Worker*. Philadelphia: Temple University Press, 1993.

Vishnewski, Stanley. *Wings of the Dawn*. New York: Catholic Worker Press, 1984.

Zwick, Mark and Louise. *The Catholic Worker Movement: Intellectual and Spiritual Origins*. New York: Paulist Press, 2005.

Index